Happy Birthday late, Roger
The reason I read this book
was because it was written by my
Nephew that is my Son's age.
It challenged me in several
areas. I hope it will be a
blessing to you. Thanks for being
my friend. Wes

Good Soil Press

Paperback ISBN: 978-1-7370394-0-2
ePub ISBN: 978-1-7370394-1-9
Kindle version ISBN: 978-1-7370394-2-6
Library of Congress Control Number: 2021910830

Good Soil Press
St. Paul, Minnesota

Cover and interior design:
The Brand Office

ALPHABETFORCHANGE.COM

An

ALPHABET

for

CHANGE

Observations on a
Life Transformed

STEVE HALLBLADE

Good Soil Press

"The COVID-19 pandemic upended many aspects of our lives. As I had to take on the role of homeschooling our non-speaking autistic teenage son, I was reflecting on all the things I wanted to teach him. A couple weeks later, our long-time friend, Steve, sent me his manuscript for An Alphabet for Change, and I knew this is exactly the kind of inner work — these attributes and practices — that I was craving to revisit and also to pass on to my son.

Steve has a conversational style, like an encouraging friend, and wants to journey with the reader toward becoming the person Christ calls us to be so we can do what he calls to do. You won't regret getting back to these twenty-six basics to nurture an authentic, integrity-fortified life."

— TAHNI CULLEN

Co-author of *Josiah's Fire: Autism Stole His Words, God Gave Him a Voice*

"I read a lot, and because I read a lot, I want to make sure the book I'm holding is worth my time and investment. An Alphabet for Change is worth your time and investment. Written as a devotional, each chapter will fill your heart, mind, and soul with the essential truth of God's word and character. The best part is that Steve lives out these attributes in his own life. If you want a daily reminder of the attributes of a godly life, if you want to be challenged to experience the fruit of the good life in Christ, or if you want a gentle reminder of the spirit of God, this devotional book is for you!"

— JOHN ALEXANDER

Executive Director of Creative Arts, Eagle Brook Church, MN

This book is dedicated to my wife, Kristine, and my two daughters, Emily and Abby. I can count on you to be supportive in all my endeavors. You continue to be my inspiration to try new things ... I love you.

To my mom and dad: You raised me in a loving home and demonstrated what it meant to follow Jesus. Thank you.

To our small group: Steve, Angie, Kendal, and Sharalee Thank you for sharpening me. Thank you for challenging me. Thank you for encouraging me. And most of all, thank you for loving me.

To my men's group: John, Barry, and Jeff Thank you for sticking with me on this lifelong journey. Words cannot express to you how much your friendship has meant to me all these years.

TABLE OF CONTENTS

TO THE READER

When I began this writing project, I made a conscious effort to invite Jesus to sit alongside me throughout the creative process. I've never authored a book before, and I wanted to make sure that the ideas communicated throughout these pages were not simply my thoughts, but inspirations from God working through me.

The idea of using the alphabet as a framework was definitely a Godsend. I literally woke up one morning with the idea entrenched deep within my mind, communicated, I believe, by God while I slept.

There are twenty-six attributes and practices outlined in this book, one corresponding to each letter of the English alphabet. I have dedicated a short chapter to each of these. My hope is that this will allow the reader to keep a narrow focus on each individual attribute.

THERE ARE TWENTY-SIX ATTRIBUTES AND PRACTICES OUTLINED IN THIS BOOK.

My intention is for the reader to take a chapter a day or one each week, much like a devotional, which will allow for a regular cadence of personal reflection time. In an effort to try to help in this regard, I've included a section at the end of each chapter entitled, "Stepping Toward Transformation." This is my way of trying to provide some practical ways in which you may lean into the attribute or practice presented.

This book is not intended to be a self-help book. All of the attributes and practices put forth in these pages are primarily built and matured in our lives through the work of Jesus Christ. To me, self-help implies that if we work hard enough and have an unwavering fortitude, we can improve these areas on our own. And while we definitely play our part in the process, I think it's important to understand that it's God who changes hearts and brings about transformation.

As you page through the chapters, you may notice one glaring omission on the list: Holiness. For me, this was a purposeful exclusion. I believe holiness is more of a journey than an attribute or practice. On this side of eternity, true holiness can only be achieved through the blood of Christ. However, growing in our relationship and union with Jesus will, by its very nature, direct us closer to holiness.

My prayer is that the culmination of the twenty-six ideas presented in these pages will leave you fixed on Jesus. When Scripture is included, you will find the paraphrase translation, *The Message*, is used. Part of digging deeper might be to look it up in other Bible translations as well such as the New International Version (NIV) or English Standard Version (ESV). I truly believe that by disciplining oneself in this Alphabet for Change and inviting Jesus to change your heart, one will begin to see transformation in all areas of life.

So ... let's get started with the letter A!

"Here's what I want you to do:
Find a quiet, secluded place
so you won't be tempted to role-play
before God. Just be there as **simply**
and **honestly** as you can manage.
The focus will shift from you to
God, and you will begin to sense
his **grace**."

— Matthew 6:6

AUTHENTICITY

[realness; genuineness]

When you think of the word *authentic*, what comes to mind? For me, it's the phrase "the genuine article," which Merriam-Webster defines as "the real thing."[1] Coca-Cola® capitalized on this definition with their slogan from 1969, "It's the Real Thing," which attempted to portray Coke® as the genuine article within the soda market. Whether it's soda, sports memorabilia, or paintings, we tend to search for and attach sentimental value to certain material possessions because of their authenticity.

Still, genuine character seems to be an elusive attribute in our world today. No place has this been shown to be truer than in the church. Role-playing has become the norm in many Christian circles. "Don't let anyone know your struggles or your faults. The *real* you isn't good enough," we tell ourselves.

ROLE-PLAYING HAS BECOME THE NORM IN MANY CHRISTIAN CIRCLES.

The trouble is, we're absolutely right. The *real* you isn't good enough, but don't worry, no one else is good enough either. This is the overwhelming beauty and grace of the Gospel! God has called us to a life of authenticity because Jesus *was* good enough. We don't need to pretend we have it all together. God already knows that we don't.

Let's look again at Matthew, chapter 6, where the apostle captures Jesus' call for authenticity so well:

> *"Be especially careful when you are trying to be good*

*so that you don't make a performance out of it. It might
be good theater, but the God who made you won't be
applauding.*

*When you do something for someone else, don't call
attention to yourself. You've seen them in action, I'm sure —
'playactors' I call them — treating prayer meeting and street
corner alike as a stage, acting compassionate as long as
someone is watching, playing to the crowds. They get
applause, true, but that's all they get. When you help
someone out, don't think about how it looks. Just do it —
quietly and unobtrusively. That is the way your God,
who conceived you in love, working behind the scenes,
helps you out.*

*And when you come before God, don't turn that into a
theatrical production either. All these people making a
regular show out of their prayers, hoping for fifteen
minutes of fame! Do you think God sits in a box seat?*

*Here's what I want you to do: Find a quiet, secluded
place so you won't be tempted to role-play before God.
Just be there as simply and honestly as you can manage.
The focus will shift from you to God, and you will begin
to sense his grace."*

(Matthew 6:1-6)

Why are authentic paintings by master artists so much more valuable than their imitations? Because they're real ... they're genuine ... they're not fake. Similarly, I believe God finds more value in our authenticity. He is not, and never will be, impressed with our facades.

I love the end of this passage. There is so much wisdom and insight to be gleaned here. First, verse 6 instructs us to find a quiet and secluded spot. In other words, get alone. God understands all the distractions and peer pressure exerted in this world. After all, Jesus interacted with it on a daily basis.

The Pharisees were the religious leaders of that day. They were supposed to be an example. They followed the Law of Moses to the letter and were believed to be above reproach. But they were masterful actors. While their outer actions seemed sparkly clean, their hearts and motives were filthy as rags. Role-playing before God is done to impress others on earth. It shifts the focus to us rather than to God. This is precisely why Jesus encourages us to find some solitude. The temptation to impress others is all but eliminated when you're alone.

Next comes the call for authenticity. Jesus is asking us to be ourselves and just be real before the throne. God not only welcomes the realness, but he is also exalted through us when we are authentic before him. Look at the last part of the verse. The focus shifts to where it is meant to be ... on God. The result is our experiencing and sensing the outpouring of his grace.

GOD IS NOT, AND NEVER WILL BE, IMPRESSED WITH OUR FACADES.

God longs for us to be authentic before him, but that does not mean that our authenticity should be an excuse to continue sinning. Paul addressed this in his letter to the Romans:

> "So what do we do? Keep on sinning so God can keep on forgiving? I should hope not! If we've left the country where sin is sovereign, how can we still live in our old house there? Or didn't you realize we packed up and left there for good? That is what happened in baptism. When we went under the water, we left the old country of sin

behind; when we came up out of the water, we entered

into the new country of grace — a new life in a new land!"

(Romans 6:1-3)

Authenticity as a believer means not role-playing the perfect saint. It's acknowledging and repenting of our struggles and failures, while striving to authentically follow Jesus.

STEPPING TOWARD TRANSFORMATION

Are you the *real thing*? Being authentic or genuine, regardless of your surroundings, can be difficult. I imagine many of us have grown up wearing different masks to "fit in." Maybe you've felt the need to be a different person when attending church than you are during the week.

Jesus calls us to a life of authenticity. He invites us to live in the freedom of his grace while striving to follow him. Take a few minutes and try to identify one or two areas in your life in which you feel you are struggling to maintain authenticity. What are some practical steps that you can take to improve?

"Never walk away from someone who deserves **help**; your hand is **God's hand** for that person. Don't tell your neighbor 'Maybe some other time' or 'Try me tomorrow' when the money's **right there** in your pocket."

— Proverbs 3:27-28

BENEVOLENCE

[charitableness; unselfishness]

Most people would probably think of the word *generosity* when hearing the term benevolence. When someone is benevolent, they typically are a generous person. However, if you dig a little deeper, you will find that there is something greater to the idea of *benevolence*.

According to Webster's New World College Dictionary, benevolence is "a kindly, charitable act or gift," but this is not the primary definition of the word.

The first definition listed is "an inclination to do good; kindliness."[1] Do you see the distinction? I would argue that a person can be generous without being benevolent. The question really comes down to the motive of the heart. Benevolence is charity or generosity that is rooted in kindness and goodness. That means if the primary motivation is a tax break or public recognition, then it is not truly benevolent giving.

Jesus was benevolent with his time and resources. It flowed out of his character; it flowed out of his goodness. If we expect to experience true transformation in our lives, we ought to be striving to align our character with that of Jesus.

Listen to what Jesus had to say about benevolence. Although he doesn't specifically name it as such, his illustration seems to embody the essence of our definition.

> "Then the King will say to those on his right, 'Enter, you who are blessed by my Father! Take what's coming to you in this kingdom. It's been ready for you since the world's foundation. And here's why:
>
> I was hungry and you fed me,
> I was thirsty and you gave me a drink,
> I was homeless and you gave me a room,

**BENEVOLENCE
IS CHARITY OR
GENEROSITY THAT
IS ROOTED IN
KINDNESS
AND GOODNESS.**

I was shivering and you gave me clothes,
I was sick and you stopped to visit,
I was in prison and you came to me.'

"Then those 'sheep' are going to say, 'Master, what are you talking about? When did we ever see you hungry and feed you, thirsty and give you a drink? And when did we ever see you sick or in prison and come to you?' Then the King will say, 'I'm telling the solemn truth: Whenever you did one of these things to someone overlooked or ignored, that was me — you did it to me.'

"Then he will turn to the 'goats,' the ones on his left, and say, 'Get out, worthless goats! You're good for nothing but the fires of hell. And why? Because —

I was hungry and you gave me no meal,
I was thirsty and you gave me no drink,
I was homeless and you gave me no bed,
I was shivering and you gave me no clothes,
Sick and in prison, and you never visited.'

"Then those 'goats' are going to say, 'Master, what are you talking about? When did we ever see you hungry or thirsty or homeless or shivering or sick or in prison and didn't help?'

> *"He will answer them, 'I'm telling the solemn truth:*
> *Whenever you failed to do one of these things to someone*
> *who was being overlooked or ignored, that was me — you*
> *failed to do it to me.'*
>
> *"Then those 'goats' will be herded to their eternal doom,*
> *but the 'sheep' to their eternal reward."*
>
> *(Matthew 25:34-46)*

So many people that read this passage instantly jump to what is being said to "the goats." Jesus' warning and ultimate rebuke becomes motivation to go on a short-term mission trip or join a service project team. Don't get me wrong, these are worthwhile endeavors, but Jesus is not outlining a checklist of things that must be done in order to receive his blessings. The checklist concept of being made right with God was already being practiced by the Pharisees and you see how Jesus interacted and responded with them. I believe Jesus' descriptions of these acts is meant to be a tangible and clear outline of benevolence.

When you begin to wrap the concept of benevolence around this passage, there is so much beauty revealed in Jesus' illustration. First, I find it interesting he uses a king in this illustration, don't you? The term *benevolent king* has been popular throughout history. It typically has been used to describe a monarch that shows regard for the benefit of his subjects, despite having absolute political power. In Jesus' story, the king is actually shining light on the benevolent actions of some of his subjects (the "sheep").

More importantly, however, is how this story conveys the matter of the heart. The sheep are bewildered and confused when the king mentions all of the kind and charitable things done for him. Why? Because they didn't perform these acts for the king but rather for neighbors, relatives, friends, and others less fortunate. They also didn't do it for reward, as evident by their astonishment at the king's proclamation. Benevolence is being charitable and kind because of the goodness and love in one's heart.

B

STEPPING TOWARD TRANSFORMATION

Generosity toward others is considered to be a noble attribute, but what if the motives behind the action are selfish in nature? Benevolence is charity or generosity that is rooted in kindness and goodness. Ultimately, it is doing things for others out of love.

What are some actionable things you could begin doing on a daily basis in order to start making benevolence a part of who you are?

"It's **criminal** to **ignore** a neighbor in need, but **compassion** for the poor — what a **blessing**!"

— Proverbs 14:21

COMPASSION

[empathy; merciful]

W hat is *compassion* and how is it different from sympathy or empathy? Sympathy really boils down to a feeling of sadness for someone else because of what they are experiencing. Although similar, empathy adds a layer of understanding to the emotions. Someone with empathy not only feels the sadness for the other person, but also experiences the emotions because of their understanding of the situation. Some have insight because they have gone through a similar occurrence in the past.

While all three of these terms are related in that they refer to one's feelings toward others, *compassion* is unique because it includes a call to action.

Compassion is defined as "sorrow for the sufferings or trouble of another or others, *accompanied by an urge to help"* [emphasis added].[1] It's really the second part of this definition that sets compassion apart from both sympathy and empathy.

COMPASSION MANIFESTS ITSELF THROUGH AN OUTWARD ACTION TOWARDS OTHERS.

So, why is compassion important as it relates to personal growth and transformation? Similar to benevolence, as well as many of the other attributes and practices that will be profiled in the coming chapters, compassion manifests itself through an outward action toward others. These are steps in both love and humility that lead to a closer union with Jesus.

One of the best illustrations of compassion comes from a story told by Jesus in the book of Luke. Although the purpose of the parable was to provide a particular religious scholar with a definition for neighbor, it shows both the emotion and the call-to-action nature of compassion.

> "Just then a religion scholar stood up with a question to test Jesus. "Teacher, what do I need to do to get eternal life?"
>
> He answered, "What's written in God's Law? How do you interpret it?"
>
> He said, "That you love the Lord your God with all your passion and prayer and muscle and intelligence — and that you love your neighbor as well as you do yourself."
>
> "Good answer!" said Jesus. "Do it and you'll live."
>
> "Looking for a loophole, he asked, "And just how would you define 'neighbor'?"
>
> Jesus answered by telling a story. "There was once a man traveling from Jerusalem to Jericho. On the way he was attacked by robbers. They took his clothes, beat him up, and went off leaving him half-dead. Luckily, a priest was on his way down the same road, but when he saw him

he angled across to the other side. Then a Levite religious man showed up; he also avoided the injured man.

"A Samaritan traveling the road came on him. When he saw the man's condition, his heart went out to him. He gave him first aid, disinfecting and bandaging his wounds. Then he lifted him onto his donkey, led him to an inn, and made him comfortable. In the morning he took out two silver coins and gave them to the innkeeper, saying, 'Take good care of him. If it costs any more, put it on my bill — I'll pay you on my way back.'

"What do you think? Which of the three became a neighbor to the man attacked by robbers?"

"The one who treated him kindly," the religion scholar responded. Jesus said, "Go and do the same."

(Luke 10:25-37)

There are a great deal of teachings wrapped up in the stories that Jesus told. True, they were simple and easy-to-understand illustrations, but they had a unique way of cutting through the ambiguity and religious fog of the day with a penetrating truth.

The neighbor was defined by his compassion. It did not matter that he was not one of the religious scholars (the priest or Levite), or the fact that he was a Samaritan, who the Jewish people had a long-standing contempt toward. No. What mattered was the compassion and love that was shown to another — and *that* is what we are called to do.

But how?

COMPASSION IS DEFINED BY OUR DESIRE TO ADDRESS THE SUFFERING WE SEE.

My brother-in-law is a follower of Jesus. He's a successful business owner, author, chaplain, and a leadership and executive coach, among other things. Many years ago, God opened his eyes to the suffering of the homeless community in Minneapolis. The sorrow and hurt he felt for these, our neighbors, led to action.

Today, he currently heads two ministries that are passionately engaged with the Minneapolis homeless community. One of these, 2.4 Ministry, prepares and serves a hot breakfast every morning (365 days a year) to those who are homeless and in need in downtown

Minneapolis. Volunteers are asked to give 10 percent of their day (2.4 hours) to help serve and show God's love for the homeless.[2] The other ministry, Threshold to New Life, is a non-profit organization that he and his wife started to "help people in the seven county metro area of the Twin Cities bridge a temporary gap in their lives." Their ultimate hope is to have people experience the grace and love of Jesus.[3]

How do we show compassion in a genuine way? I think it's important to remember that compassion starts with an emotional response to some sort of trouble or suffering we see in another person or group along with our desire to do something about it. *There should be some passion in your compassion.*

STEPPING TOWARD TRANSFORMATION

Many of us have a keen eye for seeing the suffering of others, but we are not so passionate when it comes to following the urge to help. Like a muscle, compassion needs to be exercised in order for it to grow and strengthen. Let's be honest, to step into someone's hurt or struggle feels like a risk. How will my help be received? Will it be the right kind of help? What if I get in over my head? How much time will this take? Is it really worth it? These questions can be valid, but when they keep us from acting on our impulses, they become a barrier to doing good, stretching our faith, and being blessed by the experiences.

What suffering do you see (in your neighborhood, in your community, in the world) that stirs something inside you? What if you acted on that stirring in your heart? How can you take some sort of action to help alleviate the suffering you see?

"A life devoted to **things** is a dead life, a **stump**; a **God-shaped** life is a flourishing **tree**."

— Proverbs 11:28

DEVOTION

[dedication; commitment]

What do you find yourself dedicated to these days? Is it a certain number of workouts per week or maybe a daily calorie number you've made a vow not to exceed? Whatever it is, we all make little commitments to ourselves and those around us each and every day. But these are really just goals, exercises in self-discipline, or promises to ourselves and to others. These are not things to which you are truly devoted. *Devotion* is something deeper.

Devotion is something you hope a soldier has for both his battalion and his country. During an engagement on the battleground, I would much prefer a devoted soldier than one who volunteered just to appease his or her parents.

Devotion is sold-out dedication. It's being over-the-top committed to a cause, a person, or even an object. And to me, devotion more closely resembles worship than many of the other synonyms because it involves the concept of adoration.

People can be dedicated or committed to a number of different things, but devotion requires a singular focus. Jesus points this out in Matthew 6 during his well-known Sermon on the Mount.

> *"You can't worship two gods at once. Loving one god, you'll end up hating the other. Adoration of one feeds contempt for the other. You can't worship God and Money both."*

> *(Matthew 6:24)*

In this famous sermon, Jesus is providing a warning that you cannot have split loyalties. True devotion cannot be shared in equal parts with something else. As you well know, this concept is not overly popular. We live in a world that tells us we can have it all, and it's okay to pursue selfishness. I honestly think that's why we don't hear much talk about devotion these days. We may use the word, but not in its intended meaning. I may claim I'm a devoted husband when what I really mean is that I'm a faithful husband who wants to love and honor his wife. This may seem a bit like splitting hairs, but believe me, it is an important distinction.

DEVOTION REQUIRES A SINGULAR FOCUS.

If devotion can only be given a singular focus in your life, it makes sense that it should be bestowed on that which is most important. God is the only one worthy of our devotion and worship. Devoting your life to things or causes, even if they are noble, is a dead life — like a stump — according to Proverbs. But being devoted to God, that is like a flourishing tree. What do you think of when you hear the phrase, "flourishing tree?" I imagine one that's fully

WHERE WE SPEND OUR RESOURCES TELLS A GREAT DEAL ABOUT WHAT IS MOST IMPORTANT TO US.

alive and growing, vibrantly green, and producing beautiful fruit. Now that sounds like something we all want for our lives!

So ... what does it *look* like? How can I know that my devotion is being directed toward God and not something else? I have found a couple of measurements or litmus tests that can be considered in order to help us determine where our devotion lies.

First, identify where you spend most of your time and resources. Where we spend our time, energy, and money, can tell a great deal about what is most important to us. We may say that we are devoted to God, but if we're not spending any of our time or resources advancing his Kingdom or growing closer to him personally, then these are nothing but idle words.

Second, analyze your life's fruit. We've already determined that a life devoted to God is a flourishing tree and that a flourishing tree produces fruit. So, what kind of fruit do you see being produced in your life?

> *"But what happens when we live God's way? He brings gifts into our lives, much the same way that fruit appears in an orchard — things like affection for others,*

exuberance about life, serenity. We develop a willingness to stick with things, a sense of compassion in the heart, and a conviction that a basic holiness permeates things and people. We find ourselves involved in loyal commitments, not needing to force our way in life, able to marshal and direct our energies wisely."

(Galatians 5:22-23)

These verses in Galatians spell out the Fruit of the Spirit. If our devotion is being directed toward God, this is the fruit others should be seeing in our life and experiencing in our interactions. I believe the analogy of fruit Jesus used is particularly significant. You see, the fruit produced is not for the benefit of the tree or the plant, but rather to nourish and bring joy to the people around the tree or plant. The fruit we are producing in our lives should be evident to those around us. To see if our devotion is based on God's example in Galatians, we must look to see how we're flourishing.

STEPPING TOWARD TRANSFORMATION

Where is your devotion? It's so easy to get caught up in the rat race of this world. Before we know it, we are dedicating most of our time to our job and the all-important dollar. Sometimes, our devotion is given to something noble and good, like a social justice issue. However, true devotion can only be afforded one, single-minded concentration.

Take the time to perform a self-assessment regarding your time and resources. Where are you focusing much of your energy? Ask your closest friends what sort of fruit they see evident in your life. These can be tough exercises, but the results and responses can be very revealing.

If we desire to flourish in this world and produce life-giving fruit for those around us, we must pursue and strengthen our devotion to God.

"What a God we have! And how **fortunate** we are to have him, this **Father** of our Master Jesus! Because Jesus was **raised** from the dead, we've been given a brand-new **life** and have everything to live for, including a future in **heaven** — and the future starts now! God is keeping careful **watch** over us and the future. The Day is coming when you'll have it all — life healed and **whole**."

— 1 Peter 1:3-5

EXPECTANCY

[hope; anticipation]

Hope is a word that is thrown around quite a bit these days, but the modern definition is a far cry from what the biblical authors meant when they penned the word over two millennia ago. Hope is defined as "a feeling that what is wanted may happen; desire accompanied by expectation."[1] I like the word expectation in this definition, but the word "may" does not fit with the hope to which I am referring. *Expectancy* is another word for hope, and I believe it better describes the biblical concept.

According to its usage, the Hebrew and Greek words translated to the word *hope* are an indication of certainty. It means "a strong and confident expectation," more akin to the word *trust*.[2] The authors used this word to convey a confident expectancy. It was something promised that they knew in their hearts would ultimately take place. Listen to how Paul describes this expectancy in Romans:

> *"That's why I don't think there's any comparison between the present hard times and the coming good times. The created world itself can hardly wait for what's coming next. Everything in creation is being more or less held back. God reins it in until both creation and all the creatures are ready and can be released at the same moment into the glorious times ahead. Meanwhile, the joyful anticipation deepens.*

> *All around us we observe a pregnant creation. The difficult times of pain throughout the world are simply birth pangs. But it's not only around us; it's within us. The Spirit of God is arousing us within. We're also feeling the birth pangs. These sterile and barren bodies of ours are yearning for full deliverance. That is why waiting does not diminish us, any more than waiting diminishes a pregnant mother. We are enlarged in the waiting. We, of course, don't see what is enlarging us. But the longer*

we wait, the larger we become, and the more joyful our expectancy."

(Romans 8:18-25)

Can you hear the confidence in Paul's words? This is not wishful thinking. This is joyful anticipation of a promise that will be realized. It is this same expectancy that decades earlier brought a band of shepherds and distinguished scholars (Magi) to visit a baby (Jesus) that had been born in Bethlehem.

The celebration of Christmas is my favorite time of the year. You too? All the colorful lights, joyful Christmas carols, and beautiful decorations that adorn our homes are a precursor to the celebration to come. And our celebrations and gift giving are symbolic of the gift of Jesus coming to this earth as a newborn to live among us and one day, pay the price of his life to save us from our sins.

Our family traditions involve watching specific Christmas-themed movies, listening to Christmas music daily for several weeks, and taking drives in the surrounding neighborhoods to see all of the festive lights. For us, this is a celebration of Jesus' birth that culminates with attending a Christmas Eve service at our church before we settle in at home.

Our traditional Christmas evening meal is steaks on the grill, which I admit can be a bit challenging if our Minnesota weather is not cooperative. I can recall a few times grilling in sub-zero temperatures and blizzard-type conditions! After the meal, with the fireplace in full swing, we find a comfortable spot to sit around the Christmas tree. Before exchanging gifts, we read the account of Jesus' birth as recorded by Luke.

Your family has special traditions, I am sure, that you cherish year-after-year, but it is the celebration of Jesus' birth and the expectancy of that event that stirs our souls. It's the "reason for the season" and the same anticipation that I used to have as a young boy, knowing that some of the gifts wrapped under the tree were meant for me. Now, as an adult, I have come to realize that there are far greater gifts coming — the ones promised by our Heavenly Father.

These gifts are not mere wishes that we must cling to as the world defines its version of hope. These are certainties that will come about as promised from the ultimate promise keeper. This is the expectancy that we are called to live out every day, no matter what is happening in the world. And when you do, it will not only change your outlook and provide peace, but it will also ignite in you a vision to see where God is moving.

STEPPING TOWARD TRANSFORMATION

Biblical hope is expectancy. In many ways, this type of expectancy is closely related to anticipation, but not specifically as the world would define it. It's the anticipation of what God has promised us, his followers, because of Jesus' death and resurrection.

If you could live every day of your life with this type of expectancy bubbling over into all of your experiences, how differently would you interact with those around you? What about things like worry or fear? Can they gain footholds in a life filled with expectancy? The answer is ... not very easily!

Familiarize yourself to the promises of God and live with the expectancy that they will happen. I've provided references to some of God's many promises in the appendix of this book for your reference...and for your encouragement.

"Smart people know how to **hold** their **tongue**; their grandeur is to **forgive** and **forget**."

— Proverbs 19:11

FORGIVENESS

[pardon; absolution]

Most of the time when Christians hear the word *forgiveness*, we immediately think of Jesus' sacrifice on the cross and his glorious resurrection. And we should. That ultimate act of love brought about ultimate forgiveness, atoning for all of our sin. But what about our personal practice of forgiveness? How are we doing at forgiving others, whether they be friends, acquaintances, or even our enemies? In the book of Matthew, Jesus is talking to his followers about being authentic in how they approach God in prayer. He goes on to provide an example of how they (we) should pray.

Those of us that have grown up in the church probably recognize this passage as "The Lord's Prayer." However, I would hazard a guess that very few of us could recite the very next words uttered by Jesus immediately after those verses.

> *"In prayer there is a connection between what God does and what you do. You can't get forgiveness from God, for instance, without also forgiving others. If you refuse to do your part, you cut yourself off from God's part."*
>
> *(Matthew 6:14-15)*

Did you catch that? Jesus is tying our practice of forgiving others to God's offering of forgiveness. On the surface, this would seem to imply that God's forgiveness to us is conditional based upon our actions, however, we know that we cannot earn salvation, so there must be something more to the story.

I believe that God has offered us salvation through faith in Jesus Christ. Period. This is unconditional grace and ultimate forgiveness. However, in the context of prayer and our daily walk, we are commanded to forgive others in order for that sacred union to remain strong.[1] One thing is clear, our forgiveness of others is important to God, so it should be important to us too. In his letter to the church in Ephesus, Paul offers this instruction:

"Make a clean break with all cutting, backbiting, profane talk. Be gentle with one another, sensitive. Forgive one another as quickly and thoroughly as God in Christ forgave you."

(Ephesians 4:31-32)

I don't know about you, but this seems to be a pretty tall order for me. Trying to steer clear of gossiping, vulgar talk, and bad-mouthing someone is something I can wrap my head around and work on, but forgiving someone that has wronged me, let alone doing it as quickly and thoroughly as God has forgiven me, seems almost impossible. Let's face it ... offering forgiveness can be hard to do, especially if the hurt you've experienced runs deep. That's why Mary Johnson's story is so incredible.

"Mary Johnson lost her son in 1993 after a then-teenaged Oshea Israel got into a fight with him at a party and shot him. With so much unanswered, Johnson went to visit Oshea in jail. After their first contact, 'I began to feel this movement in my feet,' Johnson told The Daily Beast.[2] 'It moved up my legs, and it just moved up my body. When I felt it leave me, I instantly knew that all that anger and hatred and animosity I had in my heart for you for twelve years was over. I had totally forgiven you.' The two now live as neighbors in the same duplex, and Johnson has even referred to Israel as 'son' in interviews.

'I admire you for your being brave enough to offer forgiveness, and for being brave enough to take that step,' Israel told The Daily Beast. 'It motivates me to make sure that I stay on the right path.'"[3]

Mary Johnson has since founded "From Death to Life," a non-profit organization dedicated to ending violence through healing and reconciliation between families of victims and those who have caused harm.[4]

I don't believe this type of forgiveness is possible without God. While it is possible to forgive small infractions, such as someone forgetting your birthday, deep wounds will require a supernatural forgiveness that can only come through God's grace.

One final thought on forgiveness. It can be difficult to forgive others if we are struggling to forgive ourselves. I know this is true in my journey. Although living with the confidence of Christ's forgiveness, there have been numerous times in my life where I have continued to beat and batter myself over mistakes I've made. It's been during these times that I have had to make a conscious effort to ask God to work in my heart to help me to forgive myself first.

STEPPING TOWARD TRANSFORMATION

Like many of these practices and attributes, forgiveness is like a muscle. It must be exercised over and over for us to grow it in our lives. We can forgive because we have been forgiven, but we must work on the practice of forgiveness.

Are you struggling from something in your past with which you have not been able to forgive yourself or someone else? Ask God to show you his love and walk with you through the journey of forgiveness. Christian counselors are a great resource, and I would highly recommend reaching out to one in your area for help.

What about forgiving others? Take time this week and ask God to bring to mind someone that you may need to extend forgiveness toward. Be deliberate at reconciliation, first in your heart, then in communication with that person if possible and appropriate.

"A **gentle** response defuses anger, but a **sharp** tongue kindles a temper-fire."

— Proverbs 15:1

G

GENTLENESS

[tenderness; mildness]

Back in the late 1960s, there was a television series that aired called "Gentle Ben."[1] The main character, Ben, was a black bear, loosely based upon the brown bear character from a children's novel by Walt Morey with the same name.[2] As a child, I watched the reruns of this show religiously. I remember being in awe of this giant, powerful animal playfully interacting with a boy about my age and thinking how wonderful it would be to have a friend like Ben.

There's a whole back story as to why this boy and his family could fearlessly interact with a black bear, but suffice it to say, the tamed bear was gentle. Don't get me wrong, Ben was still a mammoth black bear with great power, but because of his upbringing he had learned to relate to others with gentleness.

Similarly, you and I have been given enormous power. We may not weigh 750 pounds or stand seven feet tall with two-inch-long claws, but we can inflict a great deal of pain by what we say and do. Listen to how the author of Proverbs puts it.

> *"Kind words heal and help; cutting words wound and maim."*
>
> *(Proverbs 15:4)*
>
> *"Words kill, words give life; they're either poison or fruit —you choose."*
>
> *(Proverbs 18:21)*

Our words have the power to *wound, maim,* and *kill*? I don't know about you, but that sounds an awful lot like a bear attack to me!

WE CAN INFLICT A GREAT DEAL OF PAIN BY WHAT WE SAY AND DO.

What if we chose *gentleness* in our responses, both in words and deeds? What would that look like? I think it would look a lot like maturity. Gentleness is named in the Scriptures as one of the Fruit of the Spirit. Have you ever seen ripe fruit on a little sapling? No. Fruit is the result of a tree or plant that is both healthy and mature. Likewise, the Fruit of the Spirit is displayed in someone who is healthy and mature.

Unfortunately, our world is becoming vastly devoid of gentleness. No place is this more evident than today's social media. Political posts, conspiracy posts, I'm-right-you're-wrong posts — they seem to be the dominant themes across all of the popular platforms. It seems there is no longer room for difference of opinion nor cordial debate. Social media has provided humanity the means to spew our toxic rhetoric and responses at one another in an unprecedented manner. With each response, we seemingly throw more fuel on the fire, harkening back to the Proverb highlighted in the introduction to this chapter.

Gentleness calls for a different response. Remember Ben? Although he was gentle, he never stopped being a bear. Gentleness does not constitute losing one's convictions or identity. It is a matter of responding with a tenderness of the heart. It is listening to others, not only hearing them, but also looking for understanding. I believe it was Stephen Covey that coined the phrase, "Seek first to understand, then to be understood."[3] Although I believe James was relaying the same thing when he said,

> "Post this at all the intersections, dear friends: Lead with your ears, follow up with your tongue, and let anger straggle along in the rear."
>
> (James 1:19)

The bottom line is that gentleness should be a tree that is rooted in kindness.

STEPPING TOWARD TRANSFORMATION

If you're like me, the idea of gentleness can seem a bit ambiguous. I like to think of it as a response by word or deed said or done in kindness and delivered with a tenderness of the heart.

Most of us could use a supercharged boost of gentleness. If you are someone that participates in any of the social media platforms, I would challenge you to lead with gentleness. By all means, keep engaging with others, but do so with a gentleness and tenderness of spirit. As, Ryan Leak, one of the speaking pastors at our church once said, "Be quick to listen ... and slow to post."

"Pride lands you
flat on your **face**;
humility prepares you
for **honors**."

— Proverbs 29:23

HUMILITY

[unboastfulness; meekness]

Pride is the opposite of humility. True *humility* is an attribute that is difficult to find in today's world. Instead, our society wants to amplify individual accomplishment to an unrealistic level. We are all taught to emphasize our achievements, become influencers, puff out our chests, and get ourselves noticed. "Look at me" or "look at what I've accomplished" are the prevailing messages in our society and on social media today.

HUMILITY IS THE RECOGNITION OF OUR CONSTANT NEED FOR GOD.

Pride is the elevation of self, while humility is the recognition of our constant need of God and commitment to put other's needs before our own. The ultimate example of humility can be found in Jesus' life here on earth. In Paul's letter to the church in Philippi, he offers us some insightful instructions on what it means to be humble.

"Don't push your way to the front; don't sweet-talk your way to the top. Put yourself aside, and help others get ahead. Don't be obsessed with getting your own advantage. Forget yourselves long enough to lend a helping hand.

Think of yourselves the way Christ Jesus thought of himself. He had equal status with God but didn't think so much of himself that he had to cling to the advantages of that status no matter what. Not at all. When the time came, he set aside the privileges of deity and took on the status of a slave, became human! Having become human, he stayed human. It was an incredibly humbling process. He didn't claim special privileges. Instead, he lived a selfless, obedient life and then died a selfless, obedient death — and the worst kind of death at that — a crucifixion."

(Philippians 2:3-8)

Christ's example in humility is hard to humanly comprehend. Here is the creator of the universe (equal status with God) willing to become human. And why? He did this so he could live out a selfless, obedient life, die, and become a ransom for many. And while we will never come close to matching this type of humility, we are called to follow his example as best we can.

Thankfully, Paul offers some practical advice in the first few verses of this passage on what humility can look like in our everyday lives. You will notice that he first focuses on eliminating our prideful nature and then turns his attention to how we can exhibit humility in helping others. Given Paul's background and status before his conversion, I believe this is purposefully written. You see, because of his previous stature, I believe Paul understood the difficulty in being humble if there is still any amount of lingering pride residing in your heart.

So, how do we make an effort to eliminate pride so that we can walk in humility? It starts with recognizing our constant need of God. We can't do it on our own. One of the parables that Jesus told beautifully communicates this truth.

"He told his next story to some who were complacently pleased with themselves over their moral performance and looked down their noses at the common people: "Two men went up to the Temple to pray, one a Pharisee, the other a tax man. The Pharisee posed and prayed like this: 'Oh, God, I thank you that I am not like other people — robbers, crooks, adulterers, or, heaven forbid, like this tax man. I fast twice a week and tithe on all my income.'

"Meanwhile the tax man, slumped in the shadows, his face in his hands, not daring to look up, said, 'God, give mercy. Forgive me, a sinner.'"

Jesus commented, "This tax man, not the other, went home made right with God. If you walk around with your nose in the air, you're going to end up flat on your face, but if you're content to be simply yourself, you will become more than yourself."

(Luke 18:9-14)

Our world would have us believe that we must "look out for number one" (ourselves), and "if you believe in yourself, you can do anything." Unfortunately, these are sentiments that are deeply rooted in arrogance and pride. Humility begins with an understanding of who we are in relationship with God along with our constant need for his mercy and grace. Only after understanding this can we have a heart for others and a posture of humbleness.

STEPPING TOWARD TRANSFORMATION

Pride is the enemy of humility. If we want to demonstrate humility in our daily lives, we must ruthlessly eliminate our pride. We must tear it out at the root.

Are there any areas in your life where you believe pride may have found a foothold? Ask a trusted friend if they can help you identify any warning signs. Remember who you are with regards to your relationship to God. We are all sinners and in constant need of his mercy and grace. And it's normal to struggle with this because we are all sinful!

We should focus on others and their needs more than our own. See if you can make an effort to meet a specific need for someone this week. Do so without any fanfare or expectation for recognition.

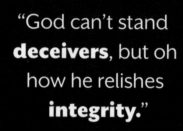

"God can't stand **deceivers**, but oh how he relishes **integrity**."

— Proverbs 11:20

INTEGRITY

[virtue; character]

"Integrity is doing the right thing, even when no one is watching."[1] Perhaps you've heard this phrase. Although it is not the dictionary's definition of the word, I love the imagery offered by this description. I believe the statement accurately portrays the true essence of *integrity*.

Notice if you will, that even in this simple description of integrity, there are three essential components.

First, there is a *moral* component, "the right thing." Ethical scholars and moral philosophers could argue the potential meaning of these words, but as followers of Jesus, we have the definitive authority. God's word provides us with a complete outline of what "the right thing" is.

Secondly, the word "doing" indicates that there is also an *action* component to integrity. It's not enough to simply know the difference between right and wrong. We must actively pursue that which is right if we are to live with true integrity.

CONSISTENCY IS THE BUILDING BLOCK ON WHICH INTEGRITY WILL EITHER STAND TALL OR CRUMBLE.

The final component is characterized by the second part of the phrase, "even when no one is watching." This is describing *consistency*. How many times have we been witness to the fall of a prominent leader because their private life did not match their public image? Consistency is the building block on which integrity will either stand tall or crumble.

Proverbs offers some great wisdom with regards to integrity. Look at these verses in the first part of chapter 11:

"The integrity of the honest keeps them on track; the deviousness of crooks brings them to ruin.

A thick bankroll is no help when life falls apart, but a principled life can stand up to the worst.

Moral character makes for smooth traveling; an evil life is a hard life.

Good character is the best insurance; crooks get trapped in their sinful lust."

(Proverbs 11: 3-6)

In each of these verses, the author is offering us a clear comparison between a life built on integrity and one that is not. Based upon these passages, it would appear pretty obvious that integrity matters. But I think it's also important to note that the consistency of moral character is not strictly defined by big decisions or substantial actions.

You might recall an occasion where your own personal integrity was questioned or weakened. So that you don't feel alone, let me provide a small example from my own life.

Not too long ago, I found myself waiting in a drive-thru line of cars at a local fast-food restaurant. When I made my way to the payment window, I handed the young cashier a ten-dollar bill for my meal. I was given the change and my meal. But as I went to put the change in my wallet, it became evident that the cashier had mistakenly given me change for a twenty and not the ten that I had used to pay.

My first urge was to pretend I didn't notice and drive off. I mean, it was their mistake, right? And really, it's not that big of a deal to the restaurant's bottom line. But it is a very big deal … if I want to live a life of integrity.

I knew the right thing to do. Had it been a large sum, the decision to return the money would have been a no-brainer. The question came down to consistency of action. Just because it was a seemingly insignificant amount, would I do the right thing? Thankfully, I decided to bring the error to the young cashier's attention. I was given the correct change and more importantly, felt much better about my choice.

CONSISTENCY
REQUIRES THE
RIGHT DECISION
IN ALL
CIRCUMSTANCES,
BIG AND SMALL.

I tell this story for two reasons. First, we must always remember that we have an enemy that will try to subvert our efforts to live the life God has called us to live. The temptation to simply drive away was something I could have easily given into had I not been pursuing my relationship with God. His nudges during times such as this are invaluable and help to keep me on his path. It cannot be overstated what kind of impression we make on others, such as that young cashier who later would have been flagged as making an error on the job, when we choose to do the right thing.

Secondly, we have to understand that consistency requires the right decision in all circumstances, big and small. If we are willing to make compromises in the small things, it provides an opening for our enemy. Over time, the lack of consistency in these small things will lead to bigger things, and our enemy will erode any integrity we've built.

STEPPING TOWARD TRANSFORMATION

*"The evil of bad people leaves them out in the cold;
the integrity of good people creates a safe place for
living." (Proverbs 14:32)*

I don't know about you, but "a safe place for
living" sounds pretty nice. I think the reason
integrity provides a safe place is because there are
no secrets to keep. Our lives become transparent
when our actions consistently match our belief of
doing the right thing.

If you're not already doing some sort of Bible
reading plan, I would strongly encourage you
to find one and dive in. *The Message* by Eugene
H. Peterson that I am using in this book provides
an easy and modern translation/paraphrase
of the Bible. If we're going to build a life of
integrity, we first need a Biblical understanding
of "the right thing."

"The **revelation** of God is whole and pulls our lives together. The **signposts** of God are clear and point out the right road. The **life-maps** of God are right, showing the way to joy. The **directions** of God are plain and easy on the eyes. God's **reputation** is twenty-four-carat gold, with a lifetime guarantee. The **decisions** of God are accurate down to the nth degree."

— Psalm 19:7-9

JOY

[elation; exultant]

I love the simple language that *The Message* provides in the verses written by David outlined on the opposing page. Look again at the first half of Psalm 19, verse 8, "The life-maps of God are right, showing the way to joy."

God has provided us a roadmap to *joy*, yet it seems as though it is rarely experienced in our daily lives. Why is that? Perhaps it's because we really don't understand the meaning of true joy.

Joy is defined as "a very glad feeling; happiness; great pleasure; delight."[1] While that may be the world's definition, it falls short of defining real joy as described in the Bible. Instead, our culture has decided to make joy synonymous with happiness, a feeling that we experience, if only on occasion. But true joy is not a feeling — it's a choice.

UNLIKE HAPPINESS, JOY IS NOT DEPENDENT UPON OUR CIRCUMSTANCES.

Unlike happiness, joy is not dependent upon our circumstances. It remains whether things are going well or not. I like how Kay Warren, speaker and author of *Choose Joy: Because Happiness Isn't Enough*, defines joy. She said, "Joy is the settled assurance that God is in control of all the details of my life, the quiet confidence that ultimately everything is going to be all right, and the determined choice to praise God in all things."[2] As Kay so eloquently stated, it's a settled assurance and it permeates from the very essence of who God is and what he has promised to us, his followers.

I believe too many of us have substituted a constant pursuit of happiness over joy. We all want to be happy, don't we? So what's wrong with pursuing happiness? The real danger is in the pursuit, actually.

You see, being happy is not a bad thing, but we need to remember that we do not choose happiness. Happiness is an emotional response to what we are experiencing. It more or less happens *to* us. Happy experiences are not constant, so the pursuit of them is guaranteed failure. Chasing it will lead to a life of ups and downs, dictated by our experiences. King Solomon summarizes it well.

> *"I said to myself, "Let's go for it — experiment with pleasure, have a good time!" But there was nothing to it, nothing but smoke.*
>
> *What do I think of the fun-filled life? Insane! Inane! My verdict on the pursuit of happiness? Who needs it?*
>
> *With the help of a bottle of wine and all the wisdom I could muster, I tried my level best to penetrate the absurdity of life. I wanted to get a handle on anything useful we mortals might do during the years we spend on this earth."*
>
> *(Ecclesiastes 2:1-3)*

Joy, on the other hand, is a choice. Let's look at part of an article published online by Compassion International titled, "What's the Difference Between Joy and Happiness?"[3]

> "Joy is an attitude of the heart and spirit, present inside of us as an untapped reservoir of potential.
>
> It's possible to feel joy in difficult times. Joy doesn't need a smile in order to exist, although it does feel better with one. Joy can share its space with other emotions – sadness, shame or anger. Happiness can't.
>
> Happiness is not present in darkness and difficulty. Joy never leaves it. Joy undergirds our spirits; it brings to life peace and contentment.
>
> Joy requires a connection. Joy is present. In the moment. Happiness mostly just passes through."

So, how do we choose joy? How do we gain that *"attitude of the heart and spirit"* regardless of our circumstances?

It all funnels back to God's roadmap. I don't believe that living a joy-filled life here on earth is possible without the Holy Spirit. Because of the advocate that God provided to us, we have been given the assurance needed to make the choice for joy possible. It cannot be shaken or taken away. This is the joy that has the power to bubble over, reach out, change perspectives, and show love and life to others.

STEPPING TOWARD TRANSFORMATION

How's your joy been lately? Do you find you're searching to experience it, or is it something that permeates from your spirit to those around you?

Personally, I've found myself caught up in the pursuit of experiencing happiness more than making a conscious decision for joy. Don't misunderstand this chapter. Joy and happiness are not mutually exclusive, but they are also not the same thing. Our opportunities for happiness are *magnified* when we are living a joy-filled life, but we cannot rely on our circumstances to dictate our joy.

Ask the Holy Spirit to remind you of God's assurances and that he is ultimately in control. Determination to praise God even during trials can be difficult. Personally, I've found worship music to be a great means of ushering me into a spirit of praise.

If you aren't sure how music influences you, try an experiment. Listen to some worship music the next time you are working around the house or driving in your car. Measure your mood. Talk to God. You might discover a new mood booster, or better yet, a new routine for spending time with God. Fill your heart with praises to him and ask for his reassuring joy to drench your spirit.

"When you're **kind** to others, you **help** yourself; when you're **cruel** to others, you **hurt** yourself."

— Proverbs 11:17

KINDNESS

[consideration; generosity]

I don't know about you, but I've always been a bit bothered by the whole "random acts of kindness" idea. Don't get me wrong, I think doing random kind acts for others, especially strangers, demonstrates amazing love and compassion. I guess the thing that bothers me about the movement is that it seems like it's meant to be an extraordinary event — one that we do for a prescribed period of time and then it's over until next time. Why does it have to be random? Shouldn't it be all the time?

I think the act of kindness should be more of a mindset, something that we practice constantly.

Like a number of the other attributes highlighted in this book, *kindness* is identified as one of the Fruit of the Spirit. If we profess to be followers of Jesus, this is one that should be evident in our everyday lives. Listen to what Paul says as he is writing to the early church in Galatia.

> *"Don't be misled: No one makes a fool of God. What a person plants, he will harvest. The person who plants selfishness, ignoring the needs of others — ignoring God! — harvests a crop of weeds. All he'll have to show for his life is weeds! But the one who plants in response to God, letting God's Spirit do the growth work in him, harvests a crop of real life, eternal life.*

> *So let's not allow ourselves to get fatigued doing good. At the right time we will harvest a good crop if we don't give up, or quit. Right now, therefore, every time we get the chance, let us work for the benefit of all, starting with the people closest to us in the community of faith."*

> *(Galatians 6:7-10)*

I don't know about you, but I certainly hope to harvest more than a crop of weeds in this life! Paul is urging us to stop being selfish and work for the benefit of all. This, by its very nature, is showing kindness. He even emphasizes that we should start with those closest to us in the community of faith, which one would think should be a given. Yet even today, I see an overwhelming lack of kindness toward one another among believers. We are short on patience and big on opinions, and the culture we live in makes it seem normal. Oh, how we need to be more careful with one another.

KINDNESS REQUIRES ELIMINATING SELFISH AMBITION AND WORKING FOR THE BENEFIT OF ALL.

I enjoy running. It is as much a therapy for me as it is a way to stay fit. It provides me a time to get alone with my thoughts as I plot my way through the neighborhoods around our home.

Earlier this year, I was running on a sidewalk through an adjoining neighborhood and I came upon an uplifting site. There, beneath my feet on the sidewalk, someone had chalked the phrase, "Be Kind" and "You are Loved." It was written so that anyone walking or running on the sidewalk could read it. A simple, yet heartfelt message.

It's hard for me to put into words the impact that those two short statements had on me at the time, but suffice it to say that I truly believe I was meant to read them that day. At the time, there seemed to be such a dark cloud enveloping our nation. The coronavirus pandemic, racial injustice, and the upcoming election were all combining to create an atmosphere of meanness and fear. I know we all remember this well. Kindness seemed hard to find and that chalk message was a small beacon of light in a dark time.

I continued to run that route quite often throughout the summer and although the words slowly faded, I was still encouraged by them during every run.

As followers of Jesus, we are to be a light in the darkness of this world. Our actions, whether we are aware or not, will either point others toward Jesus or they won't. Being kind toward others is love in action. What if our "random acts of kindness" weren't random at all, but rather part of our nature, like a fruit that is ripening over time.

STEPPING TOWARD TRANSFORMATION

If I were to ask you to rate your kindness meter on a scale of one to ten, where would you put yourself? I think most of us would determine that we probably fall in the upper mid-range. Statements like, "I'm a fairly kind person," or "I demonstrate kindness most of the time," seem to ring true for me. Maybe a seven or eight on the scale, certainly no lower than a six if we call ourselves Christians, right?

If we were graded on a curve, these scores would seem to suffice. But this is not a curve-based system; we are called to do better than that. I am not advocating a performance-based belief system whereby we should be kind to gain points or favor from our God. No. God's grace through Jesus' sacrifice is sufficient. What I'm getting at is that our response to that grace should be flowering fruit that demonstrates who we are in Christ.

Regardless of the rating you gave yourself in the exercise above, there is room for growth. Let's make kindness a priority. Think of ways that you can demonstrate kindness to those around you, both big and small. Exercise that muscle in your life and let's create a culture where our fruit can ripen.

"Jesus said, "'**Love the Lord** your God with all your passion and prayer and intelligence.' This is the most important, the **first** on any list. But there is a **second** to set alongside it: '**Love others** as well as you love yourself.' These two commands are pegs; **everything** in God's Law and the Prophets hangs from them."

— Matthew 22:37-40

LOVE

[adoration; agape]

Both Matthew and Mark share a story during Jesus'
ministry where a religious scholar poses a question
inquiring as to which is the most important of all the
commandments. Similar to Matthew's account outlined in
the verses on the opposing page, Mark writes:

> "Jesus said, 'The first in importance is, "Listen, Israel: The
> Lord your God is one; so love the Lord God with all your
> passion and prayer and intelligence and energy."

And here is the second: "Love others as well as you love
yourself." There is no other commandment that ranks
with these.'"

(Mark 12:29-31)

In each of these proclamations, Jesus is emphasizing the
importance of *love*. It's about loving God with all your
heart, soul and mind along with loving others as you love
yourself. Still, in the book of John, Jesus goes one step
further in this teaching.

"Let me give you a new command: Love one another. In
the same way I loved you, you love one another. This is
how everyone will recognize that you are my disciples —
when they see the love you have for each other."

(John 13:34-35)

In this passage, Jesus ups the game on the earlier
command to love one another as you love yourself. The
new command calls for our love toward others to be the
same as Christ's love toward us. But how can we do this?
It's definitely a very high standard, but with God's help, we
can love as we are called to love. It's pretty clear that love is
the essence of the ballgame.

All of the other commandments along with all of the attributes and practices put forth in this book are anchored in our love for God and in our love for others. Listen to how John describes it in his first epistle:

> "My beloved friends, let us continue to love each other since love comes from God. Everyone who loves is born of God and experiences a relationship with God. The person who refuses to love doesn't know the first thing about God, because God is love — so you can't know him if you don't love. This is how God showed his love for us: God sent his only Son into the world so we might live through him. This is the kind of love we are talking about — not that we once upon a time loved God, but that he loved us and sent his Son as a sacrifice to clear away our sins and the damage they've done to our relationship with God.
>
> My dear, dear friends, if God loved us like this, we certainly ought to love each other. No one has seen God, ever. But if we love one another, God dwells deeply within us, and his love becomes complete in us — perfect love!"
>
> (1 John 4:7-12)

HOW CAN WE
CLAIM TO KNOW
GOD, WHO IS LOVE,
WITHOUT ALSO
LOVING OTHERS?

In this passage, John is making the point that our love for one another is an essential outflowing of God's love for us. How can we claim to know God, who is Love, without also loving others? It is impossible.

Back in my college years, I was asked to help lead a group of high school students on a week-long mission trip to Ensenada, Mexico. Our group had been assigned the task of coming alongside a local church to build a meeting space within the impoverished community. The days were hot, and the construction work was grueling, but our team was making great progress.

About mid-week, during my personal quiet time, God broke me. The truth he laid on my heart that evening was one word: love. You see, I was completely engulfed in the tasks that needed to be completed. Whether it was pride or just the drive to accomplish our work goals, love was not present in my work. It was absent in my motivation, it wasn't being displayed to those within the community, and it definitely wasn't demonstrated with the high school students that I was leading. But that evening, in a soft whisper that seemed to recalibrate my direction, the trip changed for me.

The remaining days of the trip looked quite a bit different as our team made a conscious decision to spend time within the community. We took time to get to know the people that would be worshipping in the building we were constructing. We took breaks to play soccer and hide-and-seek with the local children. And we did our best to demonstrate love to one another and to the people we were serving that week.

I think too often we mistakenly believe that the primary objective on these types of trips is to accomplish the tasks and get the work done. And while these are important aspects of any trip, God opened my eyes to see that it is most important to show love to those we've come to serve. Love matters.

So, what does love look like? How do we show love to those around us in a genuine way? First of all, we must not fall into the false notion that love is strictly a feeling. Primarily, love is an action which can be manifested in a multitude of ways.

I think Paul provides us the best definition in his first letter to the church in Corinth.

> *"If I speak with human eloquence and angelic ecstasy but don't love, I'm nothing but the creaking of a rusty gate.*

If I speak God's Word with power, revealing all his mysteries and making everything plain as day, and if I have faith that says to a mountain, "Jump," and it jumps, but I don't love, I'm nothing.

If I give everything I own to the poor and even go to the stake to be burned as a martyr, but I don't love, I've gotten nowhere. So, no matter what I say, what I believe, and what I do, I'm bankrupt without love.

Love never gives up.
Love cares more for others than for self.
Love doesn't want what it doesn't have.
Love doesn't strut,
Doesn't have a swelled head,
Doesn't force itself on others,
Isn't always "me first,"
Doesn't fly off the handle,
Doesn't keep score of the sins of others,
Doesn't revel when others grovel,
Takes pleasure in the flowering of truth,
Puts up with anything,
Trusts God always,
Always looks for the best,

Never looks back,

But keeps going to the end.

Love never dies."

(1 Corinthians 13:1-8a)

We've probably all heard the above passage read at
numerous weddings in various translations, but I think
it's important to not compartmentalize Paul's words into
thinking it applies only to marriage. No, this is the
importance of love and what love looks like in practice
to *all* others.

STEPPING TOWARD TRANSFORMATION

Jesus has laid it out for us. The most important commandments are to love God with all your heart, soul, and mind and to love your neighbor in the same way that God loves us. I don't know that it can be made any more straight forward than this. Let's face it, as Paul alluded to in 1 Corinthians 13, you can work on all the other attributes and practices offered in this book, but if you don't love, it will all be for naught.

Showing love to people we like is easy, or should I say easier. But what about loving people that are different from us? What about loving others less fortunate or even those who have hurt us in the past? That's where it gets hard!

God is love — and love comes from God. We can really only love because he first loved us. Our call to love others is not always easy. It may take a softening of the heart, something only God can do.

Ask God to give you a special compassion for those whom you have a hard time showing love. Invite him to soften your heart and show you ways to demonstrate love to that person or group of people. Be prepared to watch for and take advantage of the opportunities God gives you.

"Talk and act like a person expecting to be **judged** by the Rule that sets us free. For if you **refuse** to act kindly, you can hardly expect to be **treated** kindly. **Kind** mercy wins over **harsh** judgment every time.

— James 2:12-13

MERCY

[leniency; clemency]

Many people believe *mercy* and *grace* to be synonymous. In fact, the two terms are often used interchangeably. One could say if you show someone mercy, you've shown them grace. However, there is a difference.

I like the differentiation between the two terms offered in *Willmington's Guide to the Bible*. Mercy is the act of withholding deserved punishment. Grace, on the other hand, is the act of endowing unmerited favor.[1] As followers of Jesus, God has poured out both his mercy and grace on us. He withholds the deserved punishment of our sin (quite literally, hell), and endows us the unmerited favor through Jesus Christ of union with him forever (quite literally, heaven).

Another way to describe the differences between the two terms and their relationship with one another can be found on the website www.christianity.com. "Mercy and grace are two sides of a coin — and the coin is love. In the author's own words, mercy is a compassionate love to the weak, and grace is a generous love to the unworthy. Humans are weak and unworthy – we all need God's mercy and grace. Mercy takes us to the path of forgiveness, while grace leads us to reconciliation."[2]

I hope you caught the first sentence. Both *mercy* and *grace* are born out of love. As it is with almost all of the attributes discussed in this book, it begins (and ends) with love.

The understanding of grace and God's unmerited favor toward us can help lead us into being more merciful toward others. So, let's turn our attention to mercy. How do we practice it? Is it even something that God has

THE UNDERSTANDING OF GRACE CAN HELP LEAD US INTO BEING MERCIFUL TOWARDS OTHERS.

called us to do?

I believe I've mentioned it before, but when Jesus wanted to teach a truth related to his kingdom, he would often use a parable, or a story, to illustrate the point. This was brilliant in that it not only drove the point home, but it did so in a way that was easily understood.

In the book of Matthew, Peter had just asked Jesus a question regarding forgiveness. After replying to Peter, Jesus tells this parable.

> *"The kingdom of God is like a king who decided to square accounts with his servants. As he got under way, one servant was brought before him who had run up a debt of a hundred thousand dollars. He couldn't pay up, so the king ordered the man, along with his wife, children, and goods, to be auctioned off at the slave market.*

"The poor wretch threw himself at the king's feet and begged, 'Give me a chance and I'll pay it all back.' Touched by his plea, the king let him off, erasing the debt.

"The servant was no sooner out of the room when he came upon one of his fellow servants who owed him ten dollars. He seized him by the throat and demanded, 'Pay up. Now!'

"The poor wretch threw himself down and begged, 'Give me a chance and I'll pay it all back.' But he wouldn't do it. He had him arrested and put in jail until the debt was paid. When the other servants saw this going on, they were outraged and brought a detailed report to the king.

"The king summoned the man and said, 'You evil servant! I forgave your entire debt when you begged me for mercy. Shouldn't you be compelled to be merciful to your fellow servant who asked for mercy?' The king was furious and put the screws to the man until he paid back his entire debt. And that's exactly what my Father in heaven is going to do to each one of you who doesn't forgive unconditionally anyone who asks for mercy."

(Matthew 18:23-35)

It would seem from Jesus' parable that showing mercy toward one another is not only something we are called to do as followers of Jesus, but it is something we are expected to do.

In an earlier chapter, we focused on the practice of forgiveness. Forgiveness and mercy go hand-in-hand with one another. When we practice forgiveness, we are also expected to be merciful in our response. As followers of Christ, who have been forgiven and mercifully saved from punishment, should we not also do the same?

Practically speaking, there will be instances where mercy is hard to see. Sinful actions will lead to consequences and punishment exists for laws that are broken in society. Yet, I believe Jesus' teaching in Matthew is referring to our hearts. Forgiveness forged in love can bring about mercy. Although a person may endure some

FORGIVENESS FORGED IN LOVE CAN BRING ABOUT MERCY.

form of punishment for a sin against us, we can still have a merciful heart toward them. It's what we are called to do.

STEPPING TOWARD TRANSFORMATION

Deserved punishment. It's something that's deserved ... they've got it coming, right? Why then should we show mercy? The answer is quite simple: Because God has shown us mercy, and Jesus has told us to do the same.

By no means am I saying that being merciful is easy, but with God's help, it is possible. Exacting punishment or harsh treatment on someone, even when it seems deserved, can lead down a dark path of resentment, revenge, and even hatred. Love softens our hearts and provides space for God to work in ways that we sometimes can't even understand.

Take time this week to ask God to soften your heart. A heart that is hardened by all of the afflictions of our world today is not capable of mercy.

"Point your kids in the
right **direction** —
when they're old they
won't be **lost**."

— Proverbs 22:6

NURTURE

[encourage; cultivate]

I truly appreciate the book of Proverbs, as is evident by many of the Scripture references in this book. The short, yet concise, statements written by King Solomon throughout the book offer golden nuggets of wisdom to my soul. In the verse on the opposing page, "point your kids in the right direction" is a call to nurture our children. The payoff for us as parents ... "when they're old they won't be lost."

The verb *nurture* means "care for and encourage the growth or development of," according to the Google dictionary offered by Oxford Languages.[1] The definition of the word brings an application that extends far beyond parenting.

Caring for one another and encouraging others in their faith journey is a practice that believers are called to engage in. There are many examples in Scripture that point out the importance of nurturing one another. I especially like the one that Paul writes about in his letter to the Thessalonians.

> *"And now, friends, we ask you to honor those leaders who work so hard for you, who have been given the responsibility of urging and guiding you along in your obedience. Overwhelm them with appreciation and love!*

> *Get along among yourselves, each of you doing your part. Our counsel is that you warn the freeloaders to get a move on. Gently encourage the stragglers, and reach out for the exhausted, pulling them to their feet. Be patient with each person, attentive to individual needs. And be careful that when you get on each other's nerves you don't snap at each other. Look for the best in each other, and always do your best to bring it out.*

> *Be cheerful no matter what; pray all the time; thank God*

no matter what happens. This is the way God wants you

who belong to Christ Jesus to live."

(1 Thessalonians 5:12-18)

WE ARE MEANT TO LIVE IN COMMUNITY WITH ONE ANOTHER.

Notice that Paul first addresses his audience as to those being nurtured. If you're anything like me, you probably have a long list of pastors and spiritual leaders that have encouraged and guided you along the way in your relationship with Jesus. Our response to these mentors should be one of extreme gratitude and love. On a side note, if you are just beginning your journey of faith or you simply have never had a spiritual mentor to nurture you, I would encourage you to seek one out. The cultivation and guidance offered is essential to bring about maturity and life transformation. We are meant to live in community with one another. Don't be afraid to seek this out.

In the second part of this passage, Paul turns his attention from being nurtured to being the one *doing the nurturing.*

The point here is that as we mature in our relationship with Jesus, we must also mentor others. The lessons that we've learned, the encouragement we can offer, these are gifts that we are called to share. And the mentorship of others can take on many different forms. Perhaps you've never thought about the fact that you are now in a position to give back, to mentor others. Don't be afraid to be that person for someone else.

My wife and I have been part of a small group in our church for many years. Our group consists of three married couples and we try to meet twice per month. Through the years, we've studied specific books of the Bible as well as read and discussed various topical books by well-known Christian authors. Far and away the greatest experience has been the mentorship that takes place within the group. Proverbs puts it this way:

> *"You use steel to sharpen steel, and one friend sharpens another."*
>
> *(Proverbs 27:17)*

There is nothing like being part of a small, close-knit community of believers who will support each other through life's ups and downs. Everyone needs a safe place where they can be both encouraged and challenged.

STEPPING TOWARD TRANSFORMATION

Nurturing others involves cultivating them to grow. It can come in the form of encouragement, challenges, prayer, and even discipline. If we intend to grow in our relationship with Jesus, having another person or a group of people to help mentor and nurture us is paramount. In turn, as we mature in our faith, we should look for opportunities to nurture others.

Getting involved in the right small group can be such a gift because of the reciprocity of friendship, trust, and encouragement that comes so naturally in these settings. Small groups can offer the nurturing your soul needs as well as important opportunities to nurture others.

If you are not currently active within a small community of Christ followers, I encourage you to start. Check with your church for opportunities to join a small group, or simply gather with some Christian friends over coffee and discuss the possibility of starting one.

"**Knowing** the correct password — saying 'Master, Master,' for instance — isn't going to get you **anywhere** with me. What is required is serious **obedience** — doing what **my Father** wills."

— Matthew 7:21

OBEDIENCE

[willingness; submission]

When you think of the word *obedience*, what Biblical character comes to mind? I immediately think of some of the early stories in Genesis. Think of Noah who was instructed by God to build a massive ship on dry land with no water in sight. I'm sure the locals probably ridiculed him throughout the building process. He may have even experienced doubts along the way, but his obedience to God's instruction was unwavering.

"Noah did everything God commanded him to do."

(Genesis 6:22)

Or what about Abram (whom God later named Abraham)?
God promised Abram that he would make him into a
great nation. He instructed him to leave his family and
country behind and go to a new land that would be
shown to him. I probably would have wanted a few
more details before leaving everything behind, but not
Abram. He simply obeyed.

"So Abram left just as God said, and Lot left with him.
Abram was seventy-five years old when he left Haran."

(Genesis 12:4)

The Bible is full of stories that illustrate this attribute and
practice, building with great crescendo to the ultimate
act of obedience, Jesus' sacrifice for us on the cross. Still,
obedience by itself is not the answer. Look at the Pharisees.
This was a group of religious scholars that not only knew
the letter of the law but also worked diligently to obey it.
Yet, they missed the mark.

There's an old hymn called, "Trust and Obey" with lyrics by
John Sammis and music by John Towner. It's a memorable
tune if you've heard it before. The title and lyrics speak to

**OBEDIENCE
SHOULD BE
OUR RESPONSE
TO THE LOVE
THAT JESUS CHRIST
HAS SHOWN US.**

the type of obedience that we are called to practice. True obedience is not just following a set of rules to earn favor or merit but is done in faith and love. As important as obedience is, it does not save us. God's grace has saved us, and obedience should be our response. Listen to what the apostle Paul writes in Philippians.

> *"What I'm getting at, friends, is that you should simply keep on doing what you've done from the beginning. When I was living among you, you lived in responsive obedience. Now that I'm separated from you, keep it up. Better yet, redouble your efforts. Be energetic in your life of salvation, reverent and sensitive before God. That energy is God's energy, an energy deep within you, God himself willing and working at what will give him the most pleasure."*
>
> *(Philippians 2:12-13)*

I love that phrase *responsive obedience*. It's a child wanting to please his father or mother, not out of fear of punishment, but out of love. It's being obedient in response to our faith in Jesus Christ and the love that he has shown us.

STEPPING TOWARD TRANSFORMATION

So what does obedience look like in our lives? I think many of us would jump immediately to the ten commandments as the clearest example of how to be obedient in our Christian lives. Let's dig deeper than that. Let's consider that there is something more.

I think obedience is aligning body, mind, and soul with God's will for your life. Jesus stated that all of the law could be summarized down to two things: loving God with all your heart, soul, and mind and loving others. I believe obedience starts here.

Take some time to brainstorm a list of ways that you can show love to both God and others. Pray about it. When you talk to God, ask him to reveal your best opportunities from the list you've been creating. Obedience is not passive; it's demonstrated in action.

"I've told you all this so that trusting me, you will be **unshakable** and **assured**, deeply at peace. In this godless world you will continue to experience difficulties. But take heart! I've **conquered** the world."

— John 16:33

PEACE

[ease; calm]

Peace is identified in scripture as one of the Fruit of the Spirit. As a follower of Jesus, this attribute should be evident to those around us. Yet why is it that worry and anxiety are increasing throughout our culture at such an alarming rate, even among believers? How can we learn to lean into the promise that Jesus offers us in John 16:33 so that our lives can be marked by peace?

2020 was tough. In the first few months of the year, a virus originated in China and spread throughout the world, creating the worst pandemic in modern history. As one would expect, the COVID-19 pandemic signifcantly raised the anxiety level across the globe. Still, it's important to understand that while worry and anxiety may be on the rise, their presence has been felt ever since the fall of mankind back in the garden of Eden.

These are arrows in Satan's quiver that are effectively used to disrupt the peace offered to us by Jesus through the Holy Spirit. Listen to Jesus' words from earlier in the book of John as he spoke to his disciples:

> *"The Friend, the Holy Spirit whom the Father will send*
> *at my request, will make everything plain to you.*
> *He will remind you of all the things I have told you.*
> *I'm leaving you well and whole. That's my parting gift*
> *to you. Peace. I don't leave you the way you're used*
> *to being left — feeling abandoned, bereft. So don't be*
> *upset. Don't be distraught."*
>
> *(John 14:26-27)*

So why does it seem that we experience a greater barrage of these arrows called worry and anxiety today? I believe one of the main reasons is due to the advancement of

WORRY AND ANXIETY ARE ARROWS USED MASTERFULLY BY OUR ENEMY.

technology. Satan has upped his game with how he delivers these arrows.

We now live in a society where we are inundated with worldwide news around the clock. Tragic events and catastrophes are happening all around the globe. With the lingering effects of a pandemic, social justice issues, and global unrest, conditions are ripe for further division and strife. Social media contributes to all of these issues and situations by breeding unfounded conjecture, conspiracies, and discord. We are left holding the pieces to a heaping pile of brokenness and stress.

Anxiety and worry suffocate peace. It happens when we are not diligently guarding our hearts. We often decide to open our hearts and take in things and circumstances that are beyond our control. The focus shifts from God and the peace that he alone can offer to us in the midst of our efforts to control the uncontrollable. The result of going it alone is an anxious heart full of worry and doubt.

So, what am I saying? Are we to ignore world events and live without compassion? Of course not. As followers of Jesus, we are called to love and show Christ's compassion to others. But we must also guard our hearts from the scheming attacks of our enemy. The apostle Paul puts it this way:

> *"Don't fret or worry. Instead of worrying, pray. Let petitions and praises shape your worries into prayers, letting God know your concerns. Before you know it, a sense of God's wholeness, everything coming together for good, will come and settle you down. It's wonderful what happens when Christ displaces worry at the center of your life."*
>
> *(Philippians 4:6-7)*

Prayer is an effective shield against worry. Paul encourages us to bring our worries to God in both prayer and praise. Turning our heart's attention to God has a way of releasing the worry and anxiety. This makes room for God's peace to settle in.

STEPPING TOWARD TRANSFORMATION

Anxiety and worry may not be the opposite of peace, but both can dramatically disrupt our ability to experience it! God has promised to give us his peace. It is the peace and calm of knowing that he cares for us and our needs. It's a peace that understands we will face difficulties, but that Jesus has conquered the world. He literally has already conquered it all. Victory has already been won!

Are you experiencing God's peace these days? If so, bask in it and let others see evidence of it in your daily life. If not, I urge you to pray about it. Cast all your worries and anxiety on Jesus and let him know your concerns. Make room for God to infuse peace into your heart.

"I'm asking God for one thing, only one thing: To **live** with him in his house my whole life long. I'll **contemplate** his beauty; I'll **study** at his feet. That's the only quiet, secure place in a noisy world, The perfect getaway, far from the buzz of traffic."

— Psalm 27:4-5

QUIETNESS

[stillness; solitude]

I don't know about you, but the practice of *quietness* is difficult for me. I think part of the reason stems from my personality. For those of you familiar with the Enneagram Personality types, I'm a seven which is named Enthusiast. I'm also an ENFP as it relates to the Myers–Briggs Type Indicator®. That personality type stands for Extraversion (E), Intuition (N), Feeling (F), and Perception (P). You can read more about either of these personality inventories, but suffice it to say, I'm an extrovert that loves to be in the center of the action!

However, I am slowly learning that my heart and soul eventually require some quiet solitude in order for me to stay in healthy communion with God.

The hustle and bustle of our world today does not provide many opportunities for quietness. There is a constant soundtrack that is seemingly played in the background of our daily lives, no matter the activity. But like an under-score played throughout our favorite movie, many of us have grown so accustomed to hearing it that we barely notice its existence. Seeking out stillness and quiet, I've come to realize, requires persistent intentionality.

SEEKING OUT STILLNESS AND QUIET REQUIRES INTENTIONALITY.

As I've mentioned, I enjoy running. Besides providing me an opportunity to try to stay in shape, it's a great way to experience some solitude. Yet, even in this solitude, I've found a way to avoid the quiet. I rarely run without my smart phone delivering my favorite tunes to my bluetooth earphones. Sure, I can argue that I need an encouraging beat to keep me on my pace, but the truth of the matter is that quietness seems a bit uncomfortable for me. Still,

I know that this practice is essential for my soul. But hear me in this so there is no confusion: quietness, in and of itself, is not the goal.

The practice of quietness and solitude is really a means of disconnecting from our everyday busyness. It allows us to be still before our Creator and commune with him. Jesus himself shows us what this looks like in the Gospels.

> "As soon as the meal was finished, he insisted that the disciples get in the boat and go on ahead to the other side while he dismissed the people. With the crowd dispersed, he climbed the mountain so he could be by himself and pray. He stayed there alone, late into the night."
>
> (Matthew 14:22-23)
>
> "At about that same time he climbed a mountain to pray. He was there all night in prayer before God."
>
> (Luke 6:12)

As you can see in these examples, Jesus was deliberate about getting alone to pray to his Father. There are plenty of other instances throughout Scripture where Jesus prayed while in the midst of the crowds, but his intentionality for solitude and quietness in these passages, as well as in the garden of Gethsemane, point to a practice worth pursuing.

There's a term often used within Christian circles to refer to one's personal time spent with God: *quiet time*. The label provides insight into the significance of the practice of quietness. Following Jesus' example, it is meant to be a time of solitude where we can be still and quiet before God to study, pray, and listen.

A few chapters ago, I wrote about the importance of nurturing. A small-group Bible study is extremely beneficial within the context of that practice because of the interaction that occurs between members of the group. In the same way, a personal and solitude time spent with God is essential in the practice of quietness.

I'm a big fan of the author and speaker, John Eldredge. As a companion to one of his most recent books, *Get Your Life Back*[1], Wild at Heart Ministries released an app called *One Minute Pause*.[2] It's based on a chapter in the book with the same title. The basic idea of the app is to provide a means of creating some stillness, where you can commune with God in an otherwise hectic day. Whether you are someone who has found a rhythm in establishing a consistent quiet time with God or not, I would highly recommend downloading the *One Minute Pause* app. I've found it to be another great tool as I continue to work on the practice of *quietness* in my own life.

STEPPING TOWARD TRANSFORMATION

Quietness is a practice that is getting lost in the noise of our daily lives. If you're like me, you probably struggle to experience moments of solitude and stillness. Developing a routine whereby you can intentionally set aside time in your day to get alone with God is essential.

Establish a quiet time and protect it from distractions. Commune with your Creator through study, prayer, and silent listening. See how building an intentional rhythm of quietness in your day will feed your heart and soul.

"You can't **whitewash** your **sins** and get by with it; you find **mercy** by **admitting** and **leaving** them."

— Proverbs 28:13

REPENTANCE

[penitence; contrition]

I f you look up the word *repentance* in a thesaurus, you will get a listing of words such as remorse, regret, penitence, and contrition. Yet all of these synonyms fail to capture the true essence of the word.

The Hebrew term used to describe repentance is *teshuvah*, which literally means "return."[1] It implies that there is more to repentance than simply regret or remorse. True repentance requires turning away from the sinful wrongdoing and returning to the life God has called us to live.

Back in May of 1998, Dr. Laura Schlessinger, a popular radio talk show personality, published a response in the Chicago Tribune to a reader's question about repentance. In the article, she outlined her belief that there are four qualities or steps to repentance. She called them "the four Rs."

The first step Dr. Laura noted was *responsibility*. Before true repentance can begin, we must first come to the recognition that we have done wrong. The next step is *regret*. It's not enough to simply recognize our wrongdoing, we must also show true remorse for the pain and problems that we have caused.

Resolve is listed as the third quality or step in the process. This relates to our commitment to turn away from the act and not repeat it, regardless of the temptations or situation. Dr. Laura goes on to identify the final quality as *repair*, which she admits is probably the most difficult. This is the crucial step of working to restore the damage we have done, as much as it is in our power to do so.[2]

Recognition, regret, resolve, and repair. I love how this unwraps the concept of true repentance. If we're being honest with ourselves, most of us would probably admit that the first two steps come easy — or at least *easier*.

WE ARE
CALLED TO BE
REPENTANT,
NOT SIMPLY
REQUEST
FORGIVENESS.

The Holy Spirit helps us to recognize our sin, which almost always translates to remorse. For me, it's the final two steps that are much more challenging. Resolving to never commit the same sin again and working to repair or restore the wrongdoing is extremely difficult. But we are called to be repentant, not simply request forgiveness.

If we look to Scripture, we can find many examples that illustrate true repentance. One of these stories comes from the life of David.

In the book of 2 Samuel, chapter 11, we read the account of King David's sin. Most of you are probably familiar with the story, but let me provide the CliffsNotes version for you here. King David, who should be on the front lines with his troops at the time, commits adultery with Bathsheba, the wife of one of his soldiers. After learning that she had become pregnant, David put Bathsheba's husband in harm's way on the battlefield so he would be killed. In 2 Samuel, chapter 12, we learn that God sends Nathan to confront King David about his sin.

Listen to words of Psalm 51. It is a Psalm written to God by David after his visit from Nathan. See if you can identify each of the four steps of repentance in this passage.

> *"Generous in love — God, give grace!*

Huge in mercy — wipe out my bad record.

Scrub away my guilt,

soak out my sins in your laundry.

I know how bad I've been;

my sins are staring me down.

You're the One I've violated, and you've seen it all,

seen the full extent of my evil.

You have all the facts before you;

whatever you decide about me is fair.

I've been out of step with you for a long time,

in the wrong since before I was born.

What you're after is truth from the inside out.

Enter me, then; conceive a new, true life.

Soak me in your laundry and I'll come out clean,

scrub me and I'll have a snow-white life.

Tune me in to foot-tapping songs,

set these once-broken bones to dancing.

Don't look too close for blemishes,

give me a clean bill of health.

God, make a fresh start in me,

shape a Genesis week from the chaos of my life.

Don't throw me out with the trash,

or fail to breathe holiness in me.

Bring me back from gray exile,

put a fresh wind in my sails!

Give me a job teaching rebels your ways so the lost can

find their way home.

Commute my death sentence, God, my salvation God,

and I'll sing anthems to your life-giving ways.

Unbutton my lips, dear God;

I'll let loose with your praise.

Going through the motions doesn't please you,

a flawless performance is nothing to you.

I learned God-worship when my pride was shattered.

Heart-shattered lives ready for love don't for a moment

escape God's notice.

Make Zion the place you delight in,

repair Jerusalem's broken-down walls.

Then you'll get real worship from us,

acts of worship small and large,

Including all the bulls they can heave onto your altar!"

(Psalm 51:1-19)

This is what repentance looks like. David uses most of the first few verses to express both recognition and remorse for his sin. In verse 6, he transitions to resolve when he writes, "What you're after is truth from the inside out. Enter me, then; conceive a new, true life." Much of the remainder of the passage deals with repair or restoration.

Still, turning away from a habitual-type sin and resolving not to commit it again can seem insurmountable. Can we ever really be repentant if we keep on sinning? I think Paul's familiar passage from Romans can help provide some clarity.

> "But I need something more! For if I know the law but still can't keep it, and if the power of sin within me keeps sabotaging my best intentions, I obviously need help! I realize that I don't have what it takes. I can will it, but I can't do it. I decide to do good, but I don't really do it; I decide not to do bad, but then I do it anyway. My decisions, such as they are, don't result in actions. Something has gone wrong deep within me and gets the better of me every time.
>
> It happens so regularly that it's predictable. The moment I decide to do good, sin is there to trip me up. I truly delight in God's commands, but it's pretty obvious that not all of me joins in that delight. Parts of me covertly rebel, and just when I least expect it, they take charge.
>
> I've tried everything and nothing helps. I'm at the end of my rope. Is there no one who can do anything for me? Isn't that the real question?

The answer, thank God, is that Jesus Christ can and does.
He acted to set things right in this life of contradictions
where I want to serve God with all my heart and mind,
but am pulled by the influence of sin to do something
totally different."

(Romans 7:17-25)

The simple answer, as Paul relates in the last few verses, is —
Yes. We can be repentant even though we may continue
to fail.

R

STEPPING TOWARD TRANSFORMATION

Repentance is a practice that God has commanded. It not only involves recognition of and remorse for our sins, but also a resolve to turn away and repair or return (teshuvah) to God.

In light of this more expanded definition, how have you been at practicing true repentance? Do you have some sin in your life that you have brought through the stages of recognition and remorse and stopped with that? Ask the Holy Spirit to give you the resolve to turn away and return to the Father. Like the story of the prodigal son, he's running toward you with arms wide open.

"A person without **self-control** is like a house with its doors and windows **knocked out**."

— Proverbs 25:28

S

SELF-CONTROL

[discipline; restraint]

I've always been one that appreciates a mystery or even a good riddle. I like the process of figuring it out, whether that be solving the crime or finding the hidden message.

Much of the wisdom offered in the book of Proverbs is presented in a straight-forward, easily understood manner. Still, there are others, like Proverbs 25:28, that require a bit more examination in order to fully grasp their meaning. What is the truth that King Solomon is trying to communicate when he makes the comparison of a person lacking self-control to a house that has had its windows and doors knocked out?

A LACK OF SELF-CONTROL WILL LEAD TO EASY ACCESS FOR OUR ENEMY TO WREAK HAVOC.

I've been chewing on this verse and praying for insight as I try to understand the comparison. Of course, there are other Biblical translations as well as commentaries that I could investigate, but I am drawn to prayerfully listen to what God reveals to me.

What does the imagery of "a house with its doors and windows knocked out," convey to you? For me, the thought of potential looting and robbery come to mind. The property is no longer secure. Any number of enemies or threats can easily gain access to the home to plunder, destroy, and otherwise wreak havoc. I believe the parallel being made here is that a lack of self-control will lead to the same result within our lives.

Self-control is defined as "the ability to manage your actions, feelings, and emotions."[1] It's easy to see how in the absence of this ability, the proverbial doors and windows of our lives would be wide open for the enemy to enter. And believe me, our enemy is real. Satan would like nothing more than to exploit a lack of self-control, whether it be in anger, alcohol, lust, finances, or any number of other areas in which we find ourselves tempted. But the world's definition of self-control does not provide us with a sufficient defense. Our ability to manage our actions, feelings, and emotions completely on our own will fall willfully short.

By now, you're probably beginning to see the consistent message being weaved throughout the chapters of this book. All of these practices and attributes have at least two essential requirements in order to mature and grow in our daily lives.

First, we must learn to rely on God. Transformation is ultimately achieved by a changed heart, and God is the only one that can accomplish that. It's worth mentioning again that many of the attributes offered in this book are identified in Scripture as Fruit of the Spirit — including self-control. As we grow in our faith, God will ripen these fruits to maturity so that they will be visible and evident to others.

"So don't lose a minute in building on what you've been given, complementing your basic faith with good

character, spiritual understanding, alert discipline,
passionate patience, reverent wonder, warm
friendliness, and generous love, each dimension fitting
into and developing the others. With these qualities
active and growing in your lives, no grass will grow under
your feet, no day will pass without its reward as you
mature in your experience of our Master Jesus."

(2 Peter 1:5-8)

The second essential requirement to bring about growth
and maturity in relationship to these practices and
attributes is exercise. If we fail to exercise a particular
muscle over a long period of time, atrophy can occur
which leads to a weakening of the muscle. Similarly, a
lack of working on (or exercising) these practices will
slow your spiritual maturity and weaken your ability as it
relates to that particular attribute. In other words, *practice
... practice ... practice.*

I would argue that this particular attribute also requires
a third essential aspect: an advocate. This is someone that
you trust to hold you accountable for your decisions and
actions, as well as encourage you to move forward. Our
advocates can be the difference between successes and
failures when it comes to reigning in self-control.

S

STEPPING TOWARD TRANSFORMATION

Self-control is portrayed by a life lived with discipline. The ability to properly control our actions, feelings, and emotions is how we think of self-control. But even though it's called "self-control," we won't be successful at it if we rely solely on self. We need to ask God to ripen this particular fruit in our lives as we mature in faith.

We all have an old sinful nature that our enemy is constantly trying to dig up and use to his advantage. This old sinful self is in constant battle with our new nature and the Holy Spirit living within us. Any lapses shown in self-control are seen by Satan as chinks in our armor, available for exploitation.

Do you struggle exercising self-control in any specific areas (alcohol, lust or pornography, spending money, anger) of your life? Perhaps you've tried time and time again to get it right, but you keep ending up in the same place. I encourage you to find a trusted advocate to journey with you. Don't be ashamed that you need support; this is a difficult journey we are all on. Embrace the accountability and encouragement in this particular area of self-control.

SELF-CONTROL

"God can't stomach **liars**; he loves the company of those who **keep** their **word**."

— Proverbs 12:22

TRUSTWORTHY

[faithful; reliable]

Would you consider yourself to be a *trustworthy* person? Trustworthiness is one of God's attributes that should drench our souls in peace. It speaks to his faithfulness and dependability. God's character, his words, and his promises are dependable. As followers of Jesus, it should also be an attribute that is evident in our lives.

A person worthy of trust is a person of high integrity. Listen to Jesus' words as recorded by Luke in his gospel.

THE TRUSTWORTHINESS OF GOD SHOULD DRENCH OUR SOULS IN PEACE.

"Jesus went on to make these comments:

"If you're honest in small things,

you'll be honest in big things;

If you're a crook in small things,

you'll be a crook in big things.

If you're not honest in small jobs,

who will put you in charge of the store?"

(Luke 16:10-12)

Notice that Jesus correlates our ability to be trustworthy in things of small significance to that of notable matters. Similar to integrity, building trust requires consistency of action. If we are inconsistent when it comes to following through on promises, even in the small things, how can we expect others to trust us in matters of importance. Even more damaging is that we learn to not trust ourselves. Trustworthiness is an attribute that must flow from the heart so that it permeates all aspects of our lives.

As followers of Christ, one of the most significant conversations that we can have with others revolves around the Gospel and introducing them to Jesus. That said, I believe that God alone has the ability to reveal his character and change the human heart. Still, his primary method of reaching others is through his followers. If we, as his followers, have built a level of trust with those to whom we would like to share God's love, the seed has a much higher chance of finding fertile ground.

There's also a noteworthy benefit that accompanies trustworthiness. In the previous passage, it's a bit veiled, but Jesus tells another story a few chapters later that highlights the perk. Can you see what it is?

> "There was once a man descended from a royal house who needed to make a long trip back to headquarters to get authorization for his rule and then return. But first he called ten servants together, gave them each a sum of money, and instructed them, 'Operate with this until I return.'

> "But the citizens there hated him. So they sent a commission with a signed petition to oppose his rule: 'We don't want this man to rule us.'

> "When he came back bringing the authorization of his

rule, he called those ten servants to whom he had given the money to find out how they had done.

"The first said, 'Master, I doubled your money.'

"He said, 'Good servant! Great work! Because you've been trustworthy in this small job, I'm making you governor of ten towns.'

"The second said, 'Master, I made a fifty percent profit on your money.'

"He said, 'I'm putting you in charge of five towns.'

"The next servant said, 'Master, here's your money safe and sound. I kept it hidden in the cellar. To tell you the truth, I was a little afraid. I know you have high standards and hate sloppiness, and don't suffer fools gladly.'

"He said, 'You're right that I don't suffer fools gladly — and you've acted the fool! Why didn't you at least invest the money in securities so I would have gotten a little interest on it?'

"Then he said to those standing there, 'Take the money from him and give it to the servant who doubled my stake.'

"They said, 'But Master, he already has double . . .'

"He said, 'That's what I mean: Risk your life and get more than you ever dreamed of. Play it safe and end up holding the bag.

"'As for these enemies of mine who petitioned against my rule, clear them out of here. I don't want to see their faces around here again.'"

(Luke 19:12-27)

Jesus' words make it fairly clear that people who are shown to be trustworthy are rewarded. In the parable, it appears that Jesus is referencing Kingdom rewards upon the return of Christ to earth, but it also holds a truth that is relevant until that day comes.

PEOPLE WHO ARE SHOWN TO BE TRUSTWORTHY ARE REWARDED.

People who garner trust from others because of the promises kept or the little things done right are usually the ones that are *entrusted* with more. More responsibility. More influence. More opportunity. This is not meant to be motivation for being trustworthy, but a gift God offers because of it.

STEPPING TOWARD TRANSFORMATION

If you had to guess, would people you know say that you are a trustworthy person? Regardless of your answer, that question is fairly easy because a simple "yes" or "no" will do. It's the follow-up question that gets to the core of the issue. Why?

We hear it all the time and it is true. Trust doesn't happen overnight. It must be built over time — block by block, action upon action. As much as we do to build it, a single betrayal of trust can topple it all and leave us back at square one. If we want to live a life others will find worthy of trust, we must learn to demonstrate our consistency of action time and time again.

We must start with the little things. If you are a person who has a hard time following through on your commitments or promises, regardless of how small they may be, pray that God will guide you in this area. It may mean showing you the wisdom to say "no" upfront, or it may be helping you persevere to meet your commitment. Over time, with God's help, you will find that the alignment of what you say and what you do will lead to faithfulness and reliability. You are building a life worthy of trust!

"How **wonderful**, how **beautiful**, when brothers and sisters **get along**!"

— Psalm 133:1

UNITY

[harmony; oneness]

I sometimes dream about what our world would look like if *unity* thrived over discord, don't you? At one time, it did. But that was back in the Garden of Eden ... before sin entered our world. In today's culture, it appears as though the flavor of the day is division. Which side of the line are you on? Who or what do you support and how can I tell you why that position is wrong?

As followers of Jesus, this kind of thinking and posturing should come as no surprise. We know that because of sin, our world is essentially broken. So, it follows that the world will propagate discord and hostility toward one another. To me, the alarming truth of the matter is that much of the division that we've seen lately is taking place among those that profess to follow Jesus Christ.

Back in the early Church, Paul wrote to the believers in Corinth to address this very topic. I can't help but wonder if his words to the modern Church wouldn't be the same if he were alive today.

> *"I have a serious concern to bring up with you, my friends, using the authority of Jesus, our Master. I'll put it as urgently as I can: You must get along with each other. You must learn to be considerate of one another, cultivating a life in common.*
>
> *I bring this up because some from Chloe's family brought a most disturbing report to my attention — that you're fighting among yourselves! I'll tell you exactly what I was told: You're all picking sides, going around saying, "I'm on Paul's side," or "I'm for Apollos," or "Peter is my man," or "I'm in the Messiah group."*
>
> *(1 Corinthians 1:10-12)*

Sure, the names may have changed, but the tone remains the same.

> "Mega-churches are just big social clubs that cater to entertaining their attenders."

> "You're one of those 'woke' Christians, aren't you?"

> "If you call yourself an Evangelical, you must vote for this candidate."

> "Do you see how he's dressed? And those tattoos?!"

> "Post-tribulation or Pre-tribulation."

The disagreements go on and on.

Paul's point and the urgency in his letter was not so much to convey that the Corinthians could not have differing

OUR DIFFERENCES SHOULD NOT CREAT DIVISIONS WITHIN THE BODY OF CHRIST.

opinions, but rather that those differences should not create divisions within the body of Christ. As believers, Jesus' death and resurrection should be the unification for us all.

Our church recently did a three-part series called, "The Divided States of America." I think the series message title speaks volumes to what we're seeing in our culture today. I applaud our church leadership in their willingness to confront and speak on issues that are relevant. The three messages in the series took a Biblical look at three topics: politics, race, and unity.

Although it could have been used in any one of the series, our Senior Pastor, Jason Strand, referenced a passage from John during the message on race. I believe it speaks volumes to the attribute and practice of unity.

It was in a final prayer for his followers, just prior to his death, that Jesus speaks these words:

> *"I'm praying not only for them*
> *But also for those who will believe in me*
> *Because of them and their witness about me.*
> *The goal is for all of them to become one heart and mind —*
> *Just as you, Father, are in me and I in you,*

**JESUS KNEW
THE IMPORTANCE
OF UNITY TO
THE MISSION.**

———

So they might be one heart and mind with us.

Then the world might believe that you,

in fact, sent me.

The same glory you gave me, I gave them,

So they'll be as unified and together as we are —

I in them and you in me.

Then they'll be mature in this oneness,

And give the godless world evidence

That you've sent me and loved them

In the same way you've loved me."

(John 17:20-23)

Let's examine this scene. Here is Jesus, just hours before his arrest, trial, and ultimate crucifixion (all of which he knows are coming), praying to God for his disciples. But not only for them. He's also praying for all believers, and that includes you and me. And what is Jesus asking for? He's asking that all believers be *unified*. Jesus knew the importance of unity to the mission. We are seeing how much damage division can cause in our world today.

If Jesus put such a high value on the unity of believers, why does it appear so absent in the Church today? And why is it so important that we fight to find it again? I love these words from author and pastor Max Lucado.

"Unity creates belief. Disunity fosters disbelief. Who wants to board a ship of bickering sailors? Paul Billheimer may very well be right when he says: 'The continuous and widespread fragmentation of the Church has been the scandal of the ages. It has been Satan's master strategy. The sin of disunity probably has caused more souls to be lost than all other sins combined.'[1]

Could it be that unity is the key to reaching the world for Christ? The world will be won for Christ when the church is one in Christ. If unity is the key to evangelism, shouldn't it have precedence in our prayers? Shouldn't we, as Paul said, 'make every effort to keep the unity of the Spirit through the bond of peace.' (Ephesians 4:3 NIV)?

Nowhere, by the way, are we told to build unity. We are told simply to keep unity. From God's perspective there is but 'one flock and one shepherd' (John 10:16). Unity does not need to be created; it simply needs to be protected."[2]

Unity is important because it fosters belief. It shows the world that we are unified because of Christ, and we will love regardless of other differences. This is essential to successful evangelism. As Max Lucado pointed out, "Who wants to board a ship of bickering sailors?"

The strategy of "divide and conquer" is being masterfully used by our enemy. Although Satan is painfully aware that he cannot conquer, he is using every tool in his toolbox to foster division. From the political culture to social media, anyplace a line can be drawn and a side can be taken ... he works it.

As believers, we need to understand that unity has already been created by God, and it is our job to keep it. It is essential to our work in evangelism for the Kingdom. We also need to realize that creating division within the community of believers is probably Satan's greatest weapon. I recently saw an Instagram® post from pastor and author Craig Groeschel that I will end this chapter with because I think it gets to the point.

> *"As Christians, we don't draw lines to keep people out,*
> *we cross lines to bring people in."*
>
> *~ Craig Groeschel, senior pastor at Life.Church*

STEPPING TOWARD TRANSFORMATION

Whether you agree with it or not, the statement by Paul Billheimer surmising that the sin of disunity has caused more souls to be lost than all other sins combined is a sobering thought. But that's the power that division can have, especially when skillfully used by Satan.

Division can split churches. Disunity can destroy movements and render someone's life witness ineffective and fruitless. If Jesus placed such a high importance on unity, that he would pray for its affirmation in all future believers, then it *must* be an attribute that we strive to practice.

Can you think of any interactions you've had recently with fellow believers where your differences of opinion have led to divisive comments? Do you commonly post to social media comments that you know in your heart will invite discord or combative responses? We have to do better. We need to model civility. The world is watching and the stakes are high.

"Good leaders **cultivate** honest speech; they love **advisors** who tell them the **truth.**"

— Proverbs 16:13

VERACIOUS

[truthful; honest]

*V*eracious is not a word that you hear every day. For those of you unfamiliar with the term, the synonyms listed above also provide the definition, according to the dictionary.[1] Truthful and honest are nice, but there's something I love about the word veracious. It adds the feeling of a vigorous pursuit of and total commitment to honesty. It just sounds stronger, more ... substantial.

I'm sure most of you are familiar with Abraham Lincoln's nickname, "Honest Abe." I, for one, prefer *Veracious Abe*, but that's neither here nor there. Although many of us know of the nickname, I would guess very few know how it came about.

WHEN WE ARE HONEST AND TRUTHFUL IN HOW WE LIVE, WE HAVE NOTHING TO HIDE.

It turns out that Lincoln was first called "Honest Abe" back when he was a young store clerk in New Salem, Illinois, long before his presidency. As the story goes, whenever he realized he had shortchanged a customer, even by a few pennies, he would close shop and deliver the correct change, even if he had to walk miles to do so.[2] I don't know about you, but I rarely see this type of honesty on display today. And when I do, it's usually in some "feel good" story on the nightly news or on YouTube®. Have our expectations become so diminished that veraciousness really needs to be this sensationalized?

Honesty goes hand-in-hand with integrity and trust.

The Proverbs are filled with verses that speak to being truthful and honest. I love the wording used in The Message for this particular passage.

> *"The wicked are edgy with guilt, ready to run off*
> *even when no one's after them;*
> *Honest people are relaxed and confident,*
> *bold as lions."*

(Proverbs 28:1)

The imagery here accurately captures the difference between living a veracious life versus living a dishonest one. When we are honest and truthful in both our words and in how we live, we have nothing to hide. There's never a need to remember what we've told to whom in order to keep the story straight. We can be *relaxed* and *confident* because there are no skeletons in the closet. Those who live with lies are living a very stressful life! We should long to be *bold as lions*.

When I was younger, and I mean much, much younger — like in elementary school — I was given the part of a young George Washington in our school's annual spring program.

The production was similar to a musical. It contained a

number of songs sung by each grade level, sprinkled with a few words by a cast of characters who were ambitious enough to memorize some lines. As one of the younger grades, we were given the task of narrating George Washington's early life. I still remember our song, "Cherry tree chop – chop – chop." And, as you might have guessed, while the song was being sung, I was on the stage acting out chopping down a cherry tree.

After the song, I was confronted by a loud off-stage voice about chopping down the tree. Then came my one and only line which I had practiced a hundred times: "It was I ... I cannot tell a lie."

BEING VERACIOUS REQUIRES LIVING A LIFE THAT VALUES HONESTY AND ADHERES TO IT.

Being *veracious* requires speaking truthfully, but there is more to it than simply not lying. It's living a life that values honesty and adheres to it. Where *authenticity* is living an honest life (being true to oneself), *veraciousness* is living a life of honesty (holding to a higher standard of truth). But these two are not mutually exclusive, in fact quite the opposite. We should learn to live authentically while striving for veraciousness. It's when both of these fall into alignment with one another that we experience true integrity.

A few chapters ago, we looked at a passage in Luke where Jesus talked about the importance of being trustworthy in both the big AND the small things. Those verses could be referenced for veraciousness as well.

Like many, I would consider myself a pretty honest person. I've always been taught the importance of telling the truth, and I rarely lie (of course, that right there is a lie). However, I've fallen into the trap of believing that just because I don't purposely deceive people, I'm honest. But what about omissions carefully left out of stories, or half-truths, or my favorite, which is something I personally need to work on, exaggerations. These are really just uniquely disguised lying techniques. Being veracious means telling the complete story — no white lies or half-truths, no misleading, no inaccuracies, and no exaggeration unless it is blatantly obvious that you are exaggerating for humor.

You see, dishonesty is a bit like a virus germ. A small, single germ on a countertop surface is not all that concerning. What's the big deal, right? But then there's another, and another, and before you know it, these seemingly small germs have created a virtual petri dish of infection. What we consider to be insignificant or small acts of dishonesty can do the same thing. That's why cultivating a life that pursues honesty and truthfulness is so important.

STEPPING TOWARD
TRANSFORMATION

Most of us know that lying is wrong. We learned it
from a very early age in the story of Moses and the
Ten Commandments.

"No lies about your neighbor." (Exodus 20:16)

But if you're anything like me, you still find yourself
struggling with the little germs of dishonesty. These
are those little truth loopholes, and if we want to live
veraciously, we must eliminate them.

For me, it has really come down to recognition. These
little practices of telling half-truths or exaggerations had
become such commonplace in my life that I didn't even
realize I was doing it. Recognition began with a prayer
asking the Holy Spirit to provide that nudge of
awareness every time I was falling into the habit.

Take a moment this week to do a bit of self-assessment
regarding honesty. Ask God to uncover any areas in
your life where truthfulness may be lacking. Commit
to striving for veraciousness and pray that the Holy
Spirit will bring recognition when you are tempted to
fall into old practices.

"Good friend, take to heart
what I'm telling you; collect my counsels
and guard them with your life. Tune your
ears to the world of Wisdom; set your **heart**
on a life of Understanding. That's right — if you make
Insight your priority, and won't take no for an
answer, Searching for it like a prospector panning for
gold, like an adventurer on a treasure hunt,
Believe me, before you know it Fear-of-God
will be **yours**; you'll have come upon the
Knowledge of God."

— Proverbs 2:1-5

WISDOM

[insight; discernment]

What exactly is *wisdom*? Can one equate intelligence to wisdom, or is wisdom something more? I believe wisdom is the discipline of choosing the right path each time we are confronted with a decision. Obviously, no one is perfect this side of heaven, but wise people tend to take the time to make good, solid choices. There's no doubt that intelligence can play a role, but it is by no means synonymous with wisdom. We've all known some highly intelligent people who have made some very foolish choices.

In James' letter to the twelve tribes of Israel, he outlines what it looks like to exhibit true wisdom.

> *"Do you want to be counted wise, to build a reputation for wisdom? Here's what you do: Live well, live wisely, live humbly. It's the way you live, not the way you talk, that counts. Mean-spirited ambition isn't wisdom. Boasting that you are wise isn't wisdom. Twisting the truth to make yourselves sound wise isn't wisdom. It's the furthest thing from wisdom — it's animal cunning, devilish plotting. Whenever you're trying to look better than others or get the better of others, things fall apart and everyone ends up at the others' throats.*
>
> *Real wisdom, God's wisdom, begins with a holy life and is characterized by getting along with others. It is gentle and reasonable, overflowing with mercy and blessings, not hot one day and cold the next, not two-faced. You can develop a healthy, robust community that lives right with God and enjoy its results only if you do the hard work of getting along with each other, treating each other with dignity and honor."*
>
> *(James 3:13-18)*

According to James, real wisdom starts by living a holy life and it is portrayed by how we relate and get along with one another. True wisdom does not exist without a God-centered life and nowhere is this more evident than in the life of Solomon.

TRUE WISDOM DOES NOT EXIST WITHOUT A GOD-CENTERED LIFE.

King Solomon is widely regarded as one of the wisest men in history. His wisdom was a gift from God as recorded for us in 1 Kings, chapter 3. During his early years as king, his wisdom provided both prosperity and a great number of accomplishments for Israel, including the construction of the temple. During this period, King Solomon also authored most of the book of Proverbs as a means of providing both instruction and wisdom to his descendants. Although written hundreds of years prior to James' description of wisdom, these passages written by King Solomon in Proverbs convey the same message.

> *"Start with God — the first step in learning is bowing down to God; only fools thumb their noses at such wisdom and learning."*
>
> *(Proverbs 1:7)*

"And here's why: GOD gives out Wisdom free, is plainspoken in Knowledge and Understanding. He's a rich mine of Common Sense for those who live well, a personal bodyguard to the candid and sincere. He keeps his eye on all who live honestly, and pays special attention to his loyally committed ones."

(Proverbs 2:6-8)

"Practice God's law—get a reputation for wisdom; hang out with a loose crowd—embarrass your family."

(Proverbs 28:7)

The above verses are only a few references, but you can see how both authors, James and Solomon, equate wisdom to a God honoring life. Unfortunately, if you follow the story of King Solomon, you will find that he begins to make some monumentally foolish decisions late into his reign. His wisdom wains as a direct result of not heeding his own words in Proverbs 1:7!

But let's get practical. What might wisdom look like in our day-to-day lives. I once had the pleasure of hearing the well-known author, Ken Blanchard, speak at a conference. He gave an amazing statistic regarding the number of decisions that each one of us make on a daily basis.

Although a few of these decisions may be significant in nature, the vast majority of our daily choices could be labeled as mundane, or perhaps even insignificant. If you're anything like me, you probably devote a great deal of energy and thoughtfulness into the major decisions that confront you. But what about the little choices? What about that car merging onto the interstate in front of you? Do you demonstrate courtesy and allow them to merge, or do you speed up to make sure you end up in front of them?

Wisdom requires us to consider every decision we make and ask ourselves the question, "Will this response or action make the world a better place or a worse place?" Put another way, am I advancing God's Kingdom and showing his love by this decision or not. For many of our seemingly insignificant choices, this may seem trivial, but I truly believe it is a discipline worth pursuing if we wish to grow

WISDOM IS AN INCREMENTAL PROCESS THAT GROWS WITH EACH RIGHT DECISION.

in wisdom. Through discipline and discernment, we can exercise our ability to make the right decisions.

With the exception of King Solomon, to whom God bestowed wisdom overnight, I believe the practice of becoming wise is a process. It begins with following Jesus and learning to live a God-honoring life, and it grows incrementally with each good and right decision.

STEPPING TOWARD TRANSFORMATION

The dictionary defines wisdom as "the quality of being wise; power of judging rightly and following the soundest course of action, based on knowledge, experience, understanding, etc."[1] As we've discussed in this chapter, the Biblical definition of the term is quite different.

My prayer is that throughout the journey of *An Alphabet for Change*, you have been inspired to work on these attributes and practices. Your roots are sinking deeper into the soil of a God-centered life. Can you feel it? That is the base for growing your wisdom and increasing your influence.

Although I have referenced quite a few verses from the book of Proverbs throughout this journey, I would encourage you to make a commitment to read through the book in its entirety. When it comes to wisdom and making wise decisions, I can think of no better resource or recommendation.

"**Help** needy Christians; be **inventive** in **hospitality**."

— Romans 12:13

XENIAL

[hospitable; friendly]

I love to sing. As I've gotten older, aside from worship or the occasional impromptu concert I give in my car alongside Spotify®, the opportunities to use my voice have continually dwindled. Back in my earlier years, however, this was not the case. During my first year of college, I sang second tenor in the choir. This was a pretty big deal for me, because of the choir's reputation and the whole audition process required. The year was jam-packed with activity, from the Christmas production to the spring tour and year-end concert.

Suffice it to say that many of my fondest memories and life-long relationships, including meeting my wife, resulted from that experience. I tell this story because there is a portion of it in which I believe God revealed to me the true meaning of being *xenial*.

The term xenial comes from the Ancient Greek word ξενία, or xeníā, and refers to being "hospitable, especially to visiting strangers or foreigners."[1] This being the case, listen to what John writes in his third epistle.

> *"Dear friend, when you extend hospitality to Christian brothers and sisters, even when they are strangers, you make the faith visible."*
>
> *(3 John 1:5)*

In this passage, John is describing what it means to be xenial. It goes beyond simple hospitality. Throwing a party or inviting someone into your home is easy amongst friends. Stepping out of your comfort zone to invite guests that are mere acquaintances, or even strangers, that is the mark of someone being xenial. This brings us back to my earlier story.

Our spring choir tour during my freshman year took place in the Northwest region of the United States. We performed concerts in Oregon, Washington, Idaho, and Vancouver, British Columbia. Throughout the entire week-long tour,

I can't remember ever staying at a hotel. It's possible that we may have for a night or two, but the vast majority of our accommodations were offered by complete strangers. These Christian families opened up their homes and invited us in, providing meals, a place to stay, and even transportation back to our tour bus the next day. The community that I felt throughout the entire experience was unforgettable. Those hosts and volunteers may have forgotten me, but I certainly have never forgotten them. They defined what it means to be xenial. When the apostle Paul was imprisoned with Timothy, he wrote a letter to Philemon in which he also mentions the importance of showing hospitality.

> *"Every time your name comes up in my prayers, I say, "Oh, thank you, God!" I keep hearing of the love and faith you have for the Master Jesus, which brims over to other believers. And I keep praying that this faith we hold in common keeps showing up in the good things we do, and that people recognize Christ in all of it. Friend, you have no idea how good your love makes me feel, doubly so when I see your hospitality to fellow believers."*

(Philemon 1:4-7)

I think it bears mention that all of the highlighted passages refer to hospitality being shown to other brothers and sisters in Christ. To me, this would seem to beg the question regarding whether or not this is exclusive or are we also called to be xenial toward non-believers, as well? Let me offer some of my thoughts on this.

These verses are all taken from New Testament books, letters really, that were meant to offer encouragement to their audience. I believe the focus on hospitality shown to one another within the faith was intentional in order to continue to build community. However, I am not of the opinion that the message is one of exclusivity when it comes to offering hospitality.

Paraphrasing Jesus, we are to love God and love others. There is no pre-requisite that defines "others" as only believers. Jesus himself practiced being xenial to all. In Matthew 14, we read about his miracle of the loaves and fishes. After a day of teaching to a multitude of people, the disciples urged Jesus to dismiss the crowd. Instead of doing this, Jesus chose to show hospitality. He fed all of the people gathered by miraculously turning five loaves of bread and two fish into a feast for all. He didn't ask anyone who didn't believe to go home before he got out the fish and the bread. No. He invited everyone to eat. And he trusted there would be enough for all.

If we follow Jesus' example, I believe the practice of being xenial must be extended to all of our brothers and sisters, whether they are Christians or not. They will know we are followers of Christ by our love — and our love speaks exponentially louder in action than it does by mere words.

X

STEPPING TOWARD TRANSFORMATION

For many of the introverts out there, the whole idea of hospitality and being xenial may be way outside your comfort zone. That said, I also believe that most of our significant growth and transformation occurs when we step outside of our bubble of comfort. There are many ways to seek out opportunities and follow through with our commitment to showing hospitality to others.

I really love the first verse referenced with the title for this particular chapter:

"Help needy Christians; be inventive in hospitality."
(Romans 12:13)

As I mentioned earlier, Paul was referencing Christians for specific reasons in this verse, however, let's look at how *The Message* translates the second statement, "be inventive in hospitality." What would it look like to put that phrase into action for others that are needy or discouraged, whether they claim to be Christians or not? Perhaps it means keeping a stack of fast-food gift cards in your glovebox, being prepared to offer transportation to someone, or having a few freezer meals saved to give away.

Take time this week to brainstorm some actionable ideas in hospitality. Be inventive.

XENIAL

"I pray to God — my life a prayer — and **wait** for what he'll **say** and **do**. My life's on the line before God, my Lord, **waiting** and **watching** till morning, waiting and watching till morning."

— Psalms 130:5-6

YIELDING

[waiting; patience]

When it comes to traffic, I think most of us would agree that the term *yielding* refers to waiting. It's being patient and allowing those with a higher priority, or right-of-way, to go first before we continue on. And while many of us have learned to adhere to this driving principle, very few of us are adept at practicing it on the "road of life."

Let's face it. In general, we are not patient people. Advances in technology have continually worked to try to eliminate the practice of waiting from our daily lives.

Microwave ovens, drive-thru windows, same-day groceries, two-hour deliveries, instant access to information on the internet ... all of these are advances and conveniences created to shorten the amount of time we must wait. With the exception of the DMV (Department of Motor Vehicles), there are very few instances where we can learn to practice patience. Although we probably didn't need these conveniences, I think it's fair to say that most of us have come to expect them and find waiting for anything to be hard.

With this as a backdrop and our world telling us that we shouldn't have to wait for anything, why should we seek to develop a yielding and patient spirit? Perhaps it can best be explained by going back to my original traffic example. Why do we yield in traffic? First, there are signs and laws dictating that we must wait. But more importantly, it's the other traffic, the other drivers, that have been given the right-of-way. By failing to yield, we can jeopardize our safety and the safety of others. I believe the same holds true in life.

WE NEED TO BE REMINDED THAT GOD HAS SOVEREIGN RIGHT-OF-WAY.

The Scriptures are given to us as God's instructions. As followers of Jesus, these are the laws and signs used to navigate through life. When it comes to "other traffic," we need to be reminded that God has sovereign right-of-way. I love what the prophet Isaiah writes in this regard.

"But those who wait upon God get fresh strength.
They spread their wings and soar like eagles,
They run and don't get tired,
they walk and don't lag behind."

(Isaiah 40:31)

More than an instruction, that sovereign right-of-way holds a promise. It's not one of mere safety, but one of growth, maturity, and well-being. Although this passage outlines that a patient spirit is definitely worth the pursuit, impatience remains a hard habit to break.

Like other learned behaviors, being impatient tends to come naturally for many of us. We've become so accustomed to getting things now, that waiting feels like defeat to us. I'm here to remind you that it's not, and in fact, quite the contrary! We should remember that the Bible specifically calls out patience as one of the Fruit of the Spirit. As such, it is an attribute and practice that will ripen and grow as we mature in our faith.

I believe one of the biggest hurdles to developing patience and a yielding spirit in our lives comes down to the need to address our self-centeredness. When the focus is on us, we will have a hard time waiting. However, when we relinquish control, and shift our focus to God, we give patience room to grow. Still, even in growth, our waiting can be tested. And it is in the testing that God's Spirit shows up. The apostle Paul sums it up well in his letter to the Romans.

> *"Meanwhile, the moment we get tired in the waiting, God's Spirit is right alongside helping us along. If we don't know how or what to pray, it doesn't matter. He does our praying in and for us, making prayer out of our wordless sighs, our aching groans. He knows us far better than we know ourselves, knows our pregnant condition, and keeps us present before God. That's why we can be so sure that every detail in our lives of love for God is worked into something good."*

> *(Romans 8:26-28)*

There's an old adage that states "Patience is a virtue," but let's be clear. Patience, or the act of yielding your spirit, is a fruit that can be grown in our lives. Demonstrating patience may be virtuous but learning to become patient requires practice and grace.

STEPPING TOWARD TRANSFORMATION

Learning to yield and build patience in your life requires intentionality, especially in a world that doesn't seem to value it. How can we expect to wait upon God if we are having trouble waiting for our dinner at a local restaurant?

Just as impatience is a learned behavior, the practice of patience can also be learned and developed. Although our own activities will offer the best learning opportunities, reading about other's experiences can also provide great insights and inspiration.

The book of Job in the Old Testament offers one of the best examples of patience in Scripture. I would encourage you to read through that book. Pray and journal as you read through it, asking God to reveal impatient attitudes in your own life. For each area that God reveals, write down some practical things you can work on in order to grow the fruit of patience and a yielding spirit. Most importantly, invite God into the journey and ask for his help to change your heart.

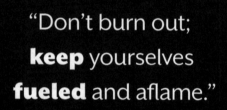

"Don't burn out;
keep yourselves
fueled and aflame."

— Romans 12:11

Z

ZEAL

[impassioned; fervent]

I have a slight suspicion that many of us who have grown up in the church may have a negative connotation with the word *zeal*. Perhaps this is due to the term *zealot*, which was often used in Scripture to describe a member of a radical political and religious sect among the ancient Jews that openly resisted Roman rule in Palestine.[1] But whatever the reason may be, we need to bury any old biases and come to an understanding of what it really means to put zeal into practice.

In the fourth chapter of this book based on the letter D, I outlined the importance of devotion in following Jesus. Zeal is an attribute and practice that builds on that theme of devotion. Where devotion is dedication or a commitment to something, zeal adds the passion, enthusiasm, and determination. The dictionary defines it as enthusiastic devotion to a cause, ideal, or goal.[2] Put another way, *zeal is the wind for the sail of devotion*. I think this metaphor provides excellent imagery of the relationship between these two attributes. Without the enthusiasm provided by zeal powering the sail, your devotion can become stagnant and motionless.

ZEAL IS THE WIND FOR THE SAIL OF DEVOTION.

As devoted followers of Jesus, we have been entrusted with the gospel. I love how pastor and author J.D. Greear puts it in an internet article called, "What is the Gospel and Why is it Good News."

> "We were dead in our trespasses and sin.
>
> Religion couldn't help us.
>
> New resolutions to change couldn't help us.
>
> Jesus, the baby born of a virgin in Bethlehem, was

the Son of God.

He did what we couldn't do. He lived a righteous
life that pleased God.

Still, he got crucified on a cross under the curse
of sin.

He did that for us.

He died in our place.

But Jesus was raised from the grave to offer new
life in his Spirit.

Jesus gives this new life to all who call upon him
in faith."[3]

This is the good news and our enthusiasm to share it
should be bubbling over into action. But for many of us,
our devotion has become dormant. We've pulled down the
sail, content to drift in quiet comfort. We have lost our zeal.

I was fortunate to have grown up in a God-centered home.
Both of my parents had a strong Christian upbringing and
they set an example for me as they lived out their faith,
while raising the family. As you might imagine, I accepted
Christ into my life at a very young age. Many of my child-
hood and teenage memories revolve around church-relat-
ed activities. One would think that with this type of background, I would have an overwhelming zeal to tell others
about Jesus. But yet, as I look back on my fifty or so years,

**TO EXHIBIT
ZEAL IN OUR
LIVES, WE
CANNOT
CHOOSE
PASSIVITY.**

I can only point to a handful of instances where I can say I was truly zealous in my faith. You know, where the enthusiasm bubbled over so much so that I couldn't help but share it. It's the kind of excitement that was often displayed by those whom Jesus had just healed.

> "Jesus urged them to keep it quiet, but they talked it up all the more, beside themselves with excitement. "He's done it all and done it well. He gives hearing to the deaf, speech to the speechless."
>
> (Mark 7:36-37)

This is the exhilaration that I want to recapture. It is with this eagerness that we are called to live. If we are going to exhibit this attribute in our lives, we cannot choose passivity. Zeal requires action.

One of the last commands that Jesus gave his disciples before returning to his Father was to share the good news of the gospel and train others in this way of life.

> "Meanwhile, the eleven disciples were on their way to Galilee, headed for the mountain Jesus had set for their reunion. The moment they saw him they worshiped him. Some, though, held back, not sure about worship, about risking themselves totally.

Jesus, undeterred, went right ahead and gave his charge:
"God authorized and commanded me to commission
you: Go out and train everyone you meet, far and near,
in this way of life, marking them by baptism in the three-
fold name: Father, Son, and Holy Spirit. Then instruct
them in the practice of all I have commanded you. I'll be
with you as you do this, day after day after day, right up
to the end of the age."

(Matthew 28:16-20)

This was a command, not a mere suggestion. Jesus was commissioning us to deliver his message to others and promising that he would be ever present as we do so. I believe therein lies the secret sauce in recapturing and practicing zeal. God will be with us every step of the way.

Z

STEPPING TOWARD TRANSFORMATION

Excitement, enthusiasm, eagerness ... these are all impossible to create on our own accord. They're attributes that result from our response to something else. Whether it's news of a baby, an upcoming promotion, or an approaching holiday season, they all begin with a stirring of emotions deep inside. Similarly, if we want to be zealous followers of Christ, and share the good news with others, it starts with emotions stirring in the heart.

I've come to realize that comfort and contentment, as they relate to my faith, often lead to complacency—and there is no zeal in complacency. In order to practice zeal, I've learned to be in prayer, asking God to stir my heart and reveal things anew every day.

If you find yourself in the same boat, I encourage you to pray for that same stirring of the heart ... then hoist the sail and catch the new wind!

FINAL
THOUGHTS

[An Alphabet for Change]

First and foremost, I wanted to take a moment to offer my appreciation and thanks to you, the reader. There are a lot of well-known Christian authors who have published some amazing devotional books, and I am honored that you have invested both your time and resources in reading this book and taking this journey with me.

As I referenced in the Introduction, the alphabet concept for this book was not my own. I truly believe it was an idea that was given to me by the Holy Spirit. I didn't have any intention of writing a devotional book previously, but after being given the idea ... I couldn't help but respond.

IT IS GOD WHO WILL ULTIMATELY TRANSFORM OUR HEARTS.

Throughout the process of writing the book, I would often receive input from others familiar with the project about attributes and practices that should be included. My approach to all of these suggestions was to listen to their input and then pray for wisdom in making a decision. In a few of these instances, changes were made, but much of the book reflects my original vision for *An Alphabet for Change*.

I can't overstate enough the understanding that this book is not intended to be included in the self-help genre. This book is more like a with-God's-help book. My prayer is that God will use the ideas written in these pages to help you grow in your faith. Of course, all of these attributes and practices require effort on our part, but it is God who will ultimately transform our hearts when we yield, listen, and act.

Now ... let's get out there in the world and show them our *love*. May your fruit mature and ripen as it clings to the vine, so that all of those around you can see and experience God's love.

ACKNOWLEDGEMENTS

As with most projects, the completion of this book would not have been possible without the superb efforts of a handful of individuals.

I am so thankful for the expertise of my editor. The insights and additions she brought to my manuscript and this process were invaluable, not only to me, but ultimately to the reader. Thank you, Heidi.

The cover design and interior layout work done by The Brand Office was in complete alignment with my vision for this book. I appreciate their willingness to understand my tone and the book's voice in their design. A big thank you to the team of Kendal, Andrew, and Derek.

Finally, thank you to the team at Good Soil Press for all of their efforts to bring this project to completion and to help me get it in the hands of you, the reader.

APPENDIX

[A Few of God's Promises]

The Scriptures are filled with thousands of promises from God. Here are just a few, highlighted to offer some encouragement. All of the promises outlined in this appendix are passages taken from *The Message*.

"Haven't I commanded you? Strength! Courage! Don't be timid; don't get discouraged. GOD, your God, is with you every step you take." (Joshua 1:9)

"Trust God from the bottom of your heart; don't try to figure out everything on your own. Listen for God's voice in everything you

do, everywhere you go; he's the one who will keep you on track."
(Proverbs 3-5:6)

"But those who wait upon GOD get fresh strength. They spread
their wings and soar like eagles, They run and don't get tired, they
walk and don't lag behind." (Isaiah 40:31)

"GOD is good, a hiding place in tough times. He recognizes and
welcomes anyone looking for help, No matter how desperate the
trouble." (Nahum 1:7)

"If God gives such attention to the appearance of wildflowers —
most of which are never even seen — don't you think he'll attend to
you, take pride in you, do his best for you? What I'm trying to do
here is to get you to relax, to not be so preoccupied with getting, so
you can respond to God's giving. People who don't know God and
the way he works fuss over these things, but you know both God
and how he works. Steep your life in God-reality, God-initiative,
God-provisions. Don't worry about missing out. You'll find all your
everyday human concerns will be met." (Matthew 6:30-33)

"Are you tired? Worn out? Burned out on religion? Come to me. Get
away with me and you'll recover your life. I'll show you how to
take a real rest. Walk with me and work with me — watch how I do
it. Learn the unforced rhythms of grace. I won't lay anything heavy
or ill-fitting on you. Keep company with me and you'll learn to live
freely and lightly." (Matthew 11:28-30)

"Here's what I'm saying: Ask and you'll get; Seek and you'll find; Knock and the door will open. Don't bargain with God. Be direct. Ask for what you need. This is not a cat-and-mouse, hide-and-seek game we're in. If your little boy asks for a serving of fish, do you scare him with a live snake on his plate? If your little girl asks for an egg, do you trick her with a spider? As bad as you are, you wouldn't think of such a thing — you're at least decent to your own children. And don't you think the Father who conceived you in love will give the Holy Spirit when you ask him?." (Luke 11:9-13)

"This is how much God loved the world: He gave his Son, his one and only Son. And this is why: so that no one need be destroyed; by believing in him, anyone can have a whole and lasting life." (John 3:16)

"Jesus once again addressed them: 'I am the world's Light. No one who follows me stumbles around in the darkness. I provide plenty of light to live in.'" (John 8:12)

"Don't let this rattle you. You trust God, don't you? Trust me. There is plenty of room for you in my Father's home. If that weren't so, would I have told you that I'm on my way to get a room ready for you? And if I'm on my way to get your room ready, I'll come back and get you so you can live where I live." (John 14:1-3)

"The person who trusts me will not only do what I'm doing but even greater things, because I, on my way to the Father, am giving you the same work to do that I've been doing. You can count on it. From now on, whatever you request along the lines of who I am and what I am doing, I'll do it. That's how the Father will be seen for who he is in the Son. I mean it. Whatever you request in this way, I'll do." (John 14:12-14)

"If you love me, show it by doing what I've told you. I will talk to the Father, and he'll provide you another Friend so that you will always have someone with you." (John 14:15-16)

"That's my parting gift to you. Peace. I don't leave you the way you're used to being left — feeling abandoned, bereft. So don't be upset. Don't be distraught." (John 14:27)

"Don't fret or worry. Instead of worrying, pray. Let petitions and praises shape your worries into prayers, letting God know your concerns. Before you know it, a sense of God's wholeness, everything coming together for good, will come and settle you down. It's wonderful what happens when Christ displaces worry at the center of your life." (Philippians 4:6-7)

"If you don't know what you're doing, pray to the Father. He loves to help. You'll get his help, and won't be condescended to when you ask for it." (James 1:5)

"On the other hand, if we admit our sins—simply come clean about them — he won't let us down; he'll be true to himself. He'll forgive our sins and purge us of all wrongdoing." (I John 1:9)

NOTES

ALL CHAPTERS

Unless otherwise indicated, all Scripture quotations are taken from
THE MESSAGE, copyright © 1993, 2002, 2018 by Eugene H. Peterson.
Used by permission of NavPress. All rights reserved. Represented by
Tyndale House Publishers, Inc.

A AUTHENTICITY

[1] Merriam-Webster Online, "the genuine article," accessed June 29, 2020,
https://www.merriam-webster.com/dictionary/the%20genuine%20article.

B BENEVOLENCE

[1] Your Dictionary/Webster's New World College Dictionary Online,
"benevolence," accessed June 30, 2020, https://www.yourdictionary.com/
benevolence.

C COMPASSION

[1] Your Dictionary/ Webster's New World College Dictionary Online, "compassion," accessed July 9, 2020, https://www.yourdictionary.com/compassion.

[2] "2.4 Ministry," Grace Church Compassion Ministries, accessed July 9, 2020, https://findgrace.com/local-compassion.

[3] "Threshold to New Life," accessed July 9, 2020, https://threshold2newlife.org.

E EXPECTANCY

[1] Your Dictionary/Webster's New World College Dictionary Online, "expectancy," accessed July 21, 2020, https://www.yourdictionary.com/expectancy#websters.

[2] Bible.org, "Hope," accessed July 21,2020, https://bible.org/article/hope.

F FORGIVENESS

[1] Steffen, Daniel S, "Is Divine Forgiveness Conditional Or Unconditional In The Gospel Of Matthew?" Bible.org, March 12, 2013, accessed July 28, 2020, https://bible.org/article/divine-forgiveness-conditional-or-unconditional-gospel-matthew.

[2] Isay, Dave, "You Killed My Son … And I Forgive You," The Daily Beast, October 23, 2013, accessed July 28, 2020, https://www.thedailybeast.com/you-killed-my-sonand-i-forgive-you.

[3] LaBianaca, Juliana, "10 Inspiring Stories of Extreme Forgiveness That Will Lift Your Spirits: An Unlikely Friendship," Reader's Digest, last updated August 30, 2017, accessed July 28, 2020, https://www.rd.com/list/inspiring-forgiveness-stories/.

[4] Israel, Oshea and Johnson, Mary, "Our Mission," From Death to Life, accessed July 28, 2020, http://www.fromdeathtolife.us/home.html.

G GENTLENESS

[1] Gentle Ben, Miami: Ivan Tors Production/CBS Television Network, 1967-1969.

[2] Morey, Walt, Gentle Ben, New York City: E.P. Dutton, 1965.

[3] Covey, Steven. The 7 Habits of Highly Effective People, New York City: Free Press Publishing, 1989.

I INTEGRITY

[1] According to C.S. Lewis Foundation, this is a quote often attributed to C.S. Lewis, however, it is actually a paraphrase from Charles W. Marshall as quoted in Shattering the Glass Slipper. Prominent Publishing, 2003, accessed August 6, 2020, http://www.cslewis.org/aboutus/faq/quotes-misattributed/.

J JOY

[1] Your Dictionary/Webster's New World College Dictionary Online, "joy," accessed August 13, 2020, https://www.yourdictionary.com/joy.

[2] Warren, Kay. Choose Joy: Because Happiness Isn't Enough, Grand Rapids, Michigan: Revell, 2012.

[3] "What's the Difference Between Joy and Happiness," Compassion International, accessed August 13, 2020, https://www.compassion.com/sponsor_a_child/difference-between-joy-and-happiness.htm.

M MERCY

[1] Willmington, H.L. Willmington's Guide to the Bible, Carol Stream, Illinois: Tyndale House, 1981.

[2] Wijaya, Philip. "What Is the Difference Between Grace and Mercy?" Christianity.com, accessed 27 August 2020, https://www.christianity.com/wiki/christian-terms/what-is-the-difference-between-grace-and-mercy.html.

N NURTURE

[1] Google and Oxford Languages Online, "nurture," accessed September 3, 2020, https://languages.oup.com/google-dictionary-en.

Q QUIETNESS

[1] Eldredge, John, Get Your Life Back: Everyday Practices for a World Gone Mad, Nashville: Thomas Nelson Publishing, 2020.

[2] One Minute Pause mobile phone app, Wild at Heart Ministries/ Ransomed Heart Ministries, used with permission, version 9.0.0, January 2021.

R REPENTANCE

[1] Lawrence, Natan, "Teshuvah: A Word YOU Need to Add to YOUR Lexicon," hoshanarabbah.org, accessed September 15, 2020, https:// hoshanarabbah.org/blog/2013/08/03/teshuvah/.

[2] Schlessinger, Dr. Laura, "4 Steps to Repentence," The Chicago Tribune/ New York Times Special Features, accessed September 15, 2020, https:// www.chicagotribune.com/news/ct-xpm-1998-05-10-9805100475-story. html.

S SELF-CONTROL

[1] Your Dictionary/English Wiktionary Online, "self-control," accessed September 22, 2020, https://www.yourdictionary.com/self-control.

U UNITY

[1] Billheimer, Paul E. Love Covers: A Biblical Design for Unity in the Body of Christ. Minneapolis: Bethany House, 1981.

[2] Lucado, Max, "Pray for Unity," MaxLucado.com, accessed October 6, 2020, https://maxlucado.com/pray-for-unity.

V VERACIOUS

[1] Your Dictionary/The American Heritage Dictionary Online, "veracious," accessed October 20, 2020, https://www.yourdictionary.com/veracious.

[2] Leidner, Gordon, "Lincoln's Honesty," Great American History, accessed October 20, 2020, https://greatamericanhistory.net/honesty.htm.

W WISDOM

[1] Your Dictionary/Webster's New World College Dictionary Online, "wisdom," accessed October 27, 2020, https://www.yourdictionary.com/wisdom.

X XENIAL

[1] Your Dictionary/Wiktionary Online, "xenial," accessed October 29, 2020, https://en.wiktionary.org/w/index.php?title=xenial&oldid=59647624.

Z ZEAL

[1] Your Dictionary/Webster's New World College Dictionary Online, "zealot," accessed November 4, 2020, https://www.yourdictionary.com/zealot.

[2] Your Dictionary/The American Heritage® Dictionary Online, "zeal," accessed November 4, 2020, https://www.yourdictionary.com/zeal.

[3] Greear, J.D, "What Is the Gospel and Why Is it Good News?" Crosswalk.com, accessed November 4, 2020, https://www.crosswalk.com/faith/bible-study/what-is-the-gospel-and-why-is-it-good-news.html.

CPSIA information can be obtained
at www.ICGtesting.com
Printed in the USA
LVHW011048040621
689359LV00016B/1208